HAUNTED
HISTORY
OF
DELAWARE

HAUNTED HISTORY
OF
DELAWARE

JOSH HITCHENS

HAUNTED
America

Published by Haunted America
A Division of The History Press
Charleston, SC
www.historypress.com

Unless otherwise noted, photographs were taken by the author.

First published 2021

ISBN 9781540248695

Library of Congress Control Number: 2021937134

Notice: The information in this book is true and complete to the best of our knowledge. It is offered without guarantee on the part of the author or The History Press. The author and The History Press disclaim all liability in connection with the use of this book.

*This book is dedicated to all my family, the living
and the dead, and especially in memory of*

*Uncle Ralph Lewis Hitchens Jr.
May 23, 1955–February 17, 2020
who would have loved this book*

and

For Jacob Glickman, without whom this book would never have been written

and

*For Eileen Reeser, the Ghost Lady of Philadelphia
who gave me the gift of telling ghost stories for a living*

CONTENTS

Acknowledgements   9
Introduction: Gather Round My Campfire   13

1. Phantoms at Fort Delaware   21
2. Rockwood Mansion Revenants   35
3. The Screaming Lady of Lums Pond   47
4. A Headless Horseman in Newark   52
5. The Legend of Fiddler's Bridge   58
6. Dark Entities on Dover Green   65
7. Four Wraiths at Woodburn   70
8. The Vanishing Boardwalk   77
9. The Skull in the Scarlet Hatbox   82
10. A Haunted History of Lewes   94
11. Bumps in the Night on Bethany Beach   106
12. Maggie, I Have Your Baby   113
13. Wicked Witches and Swamp Monsters   119
14. Ghostly Guardians at Old Christ Church   126

Epilogue: The Most Haunted House in Delaware   133
Bibliography   139
About the Author   141

ACKNOWLEDGEMENTS

N o one writes a book alone, and I have many people to thank for making the volume you hold in your hands a reality. First and foremost are Kate Jenkins and Abigail Fleming, my editors at The History Press, who guided me through this process with consummate skill and support.

I also am immensely grateful for the assistance of many people and organizations who took the time to speak with me during the writing of this book, providing invaluable historic background and, in some cases, their own personal stories. You will find all their names throughout the following pages, but I would particularly like to thank the Delaware Public Archives, Rick and Alice Loveless of the Rockwood Paranormal Experience Team and Stacy Northam-Smith and everyone at the Old Christ Church League. I am especially grateful to Jacob Glickman and Ryan Walter, both of whom took time out of their busy schedules to drive me to locations up and down the First State for research and adventure. Finally, from my heart, I would like to thank all my friends who believed I could do this. I truly could not have done this without you—all of you.

In collecting and retelling these tales, I stand on the shoulders of the historians and folklorists who have come before me. John Lofland, the eccentric and prolific "Milford Bard" who was friends with Edgar Allan Poe, is one of the earliest to write down many of the state's stories in print. The Federal Writers' Project preserved an astonishing amount of folklore and history in its 1938 book *Delaware: A Guide to the First State*, an invaluable resource. Dorothy Williams Pepper devoted her life to recounting local legends and lore, most notably in her extraordinary 1976 book *Folklore of Sussex County, Delaware*, and unwittingly became part of one of the state's spookiest legends herself. I must also pay tribute to a true giant of Delaware ghost stories, Ed Okonowicz. I can think of no other writer who has done more to document and preserve the creepy corners of the First State's history than Ed. His nine-volume *Spirits Between the Bays* book series imagines the Delmarva Peninsula as a giant haunted house, with titles such as *Pulling Back the Curtain, Opening the Door, Welcome Inn* and more. Ed Okonowicz is a master storyteller, and I encourage everyone to seek out his substantial body of work. Other authors, including Mindie Burgoyne, Pam George, David Healey and Michael Morgan, have all written numerous excellent books about the history and legends of the Eastern Shore published by The History Press, and I feel deeply honored and humbled to be in their company.

The search for the hidden items of Delaware history is an elusive quest—at once a source of charm and despair. He who seeks for knowledge outside the beaten path must himself be a pioneer, go back to original sources and bit by bit piece his picture together like a fragment of literary mosaic.
—*Judge Richard S. Rodney,* Colonial Finances in Delaware, *1928*

The songs men sang, the yarns they spun, and the words they used to express themselves are of such a fragile and informal nature that they are easily lost and forgotten. This is what folklore is all about: an unstructured oral tradition handed down from generation to generation. As history, of course, it isn't dependable. But what it lacks in precision and documentation, it compensates by injecting vivacity, color, and charm.
—*M. Catherine Downing and Edward L. Fowler,* Folklore of Sussex County, Delaware, *1976*

GATHER ROUND MY CAMPFIRE

G ood evening, my friend. I have been waiting for you here, in the night, in the dark. I built a campfire to help the spirits find us. Welcome to the *Haunted History of Delaware*. I hope it is midnight wherever you are right now, for that is the best time of all to tell a tale of terror. Imagine that it is the witching hour and turn the lights down low, as low as you can and still read these words. I saved a spot around my campfire just for you. Sit with me here, in the shadows of this ancient, haunted forest, around these flickering flames. I have so many stories to tell you before the sun comes up. Come close to me and listen…if you dare.

My name is Josh Hitchens, and I tell ghost stories for a living. Since 2007, I have been a professional storyteller for the Ghost Tour of Philadelphia, the extremely historic and extremely haunted city I have lived in for eighteen years as of this writing. However, the state of Delaware will always be the place I truly call home. I was born and raised in Sussex County. Branches of my family tree have lived in the state for centuries, as they still do today. A little country intersection within the woods of Sussex County is named Hitchens Crossroads in honor of my ancestors who made homes around there in times gone by. The Laurel Historical Society is currently restoring the Hitchens Homestead, a rural Gothic Revival cottage built in 1878 and occupied by six generations of my family, to become a local living history site and museum.

INTRODUCTION

As I grew up among the plentiful farmland and ever-present woods surrounding my childhood home and possessed a vivid imagination from an early age, Delaware's haunted history has always felt extraordinarily present and alive to me. There are buildings standing silently in the forests that date back as far as the seventeenth century. Among the fields of corn, soybeans and chicken houses, you will sometimes find lonely, weed-choked family graveyards long abandoned. And at night, as you drive in your car along the isolated, quiet country roads, you begin to wonder what strange things might be lurking behind the tall masses of trees, waiting for you in the dark.

When I was about eight years old, my grandparents took me on my first ghost tour. It was in Williamsburg, Virginia. Like Delaware, it is a perfect place for ghost stories. You are away from the modern world completely. It is pitch black dark, except for the single white candle in the storyteller's lantern. She walks us through the fields, the streets, to the fronts of old landmarks. You could be in any time. It could be centuries ago. And as you listen to the ghost stories, told quietly in the dark, you begin to feel the tingling of fear starting in the pit of your stomach. Because, of course, there *are* ghosts in these houses, there *are* ghosts all around you, and at any second you might see the apparition of the man running barefoot out of the woods right toward you, coming for you. Then you look at the windows of the deserted mansion, feeling absolutely certain that any moment now you will see the Face looking out at you, that terrible face that you've seen in your nightmares since you were young, something right in front of you that's been dead for a very long time. Sometimes you never see the face. But sometimes, you do. By the end of that ghost tour, I knew what I wanted to be when I grew up. And here we are.

I take great pride in saying at the beginning of my ghost tour in Philadelphia, "I am not a paranormal investigator. I am a storyteller." I believe there is a great power in that, of knowing that you are part of a chain that goes back through the ages, ever since we learned to talk and sit around a fire, telling stories to one another in the dark. And ghost stories are always the best. When you feel truly afraid, you know you are alive. That moment when you were truly, deeply frightened can burn itself into your memory forever. Years later you can recall every sensory detail, and you get the chill again, and you shiver. That is what a ghost story can do, if the telling is good. The receiving and passing on of ghost stories and legends is, to me, the best and most enjoyable gateway into discovering the hidden riches of local history, no matter where you live.

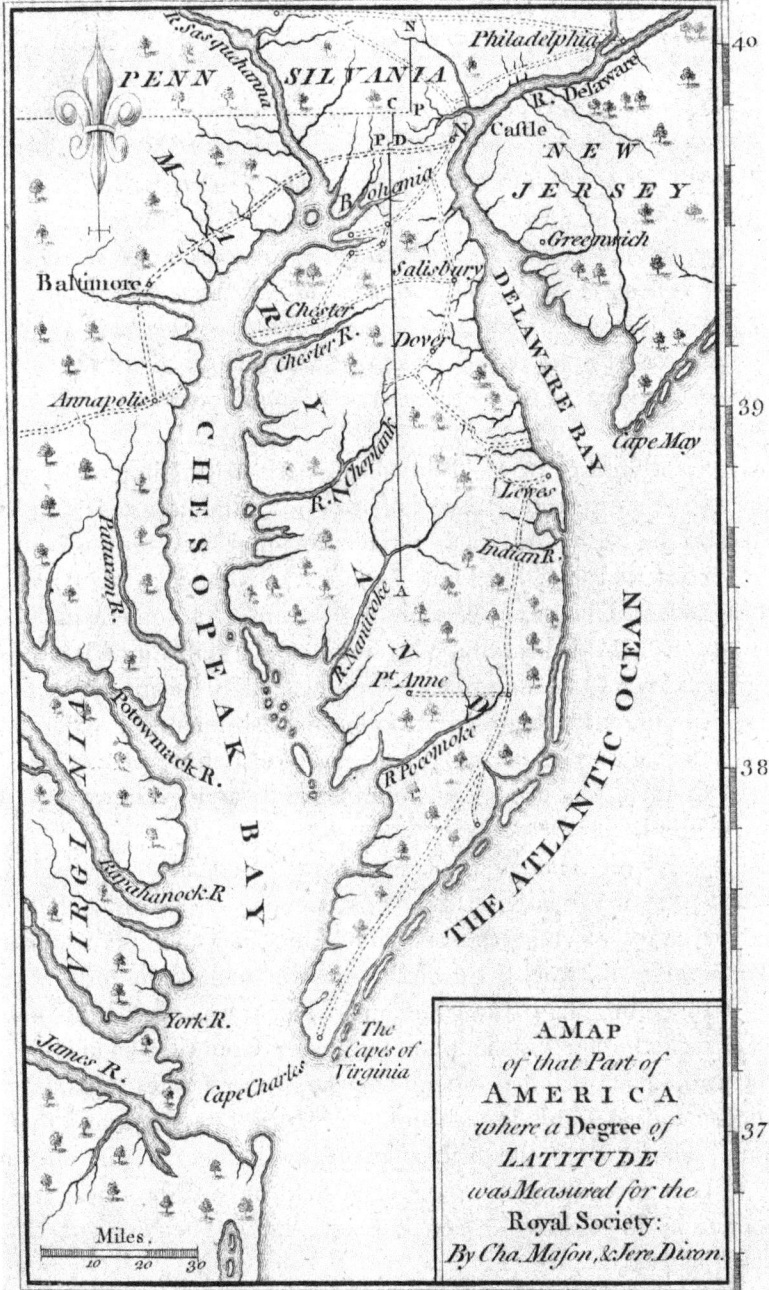

A map of the Delmarva Peninsula as it appeared in 1769. *Delaware Public Archives.*

INTRODUCTION

The Federal Writers' Project's exhaustive and deliciously readable 1938 book *Delaware: A Guide to the First State*, begins like this:

"Delaware is like a diamond, diminutive, but having within it inherent value," the Milford Bard, John Lofland, wrote in 1847. This was perhaps the origin of Delaware's popular name, the Diamond State. But it may have come from Thomas Jefferson's reference to Delaware as "a jewel among the states," probably because of its compact area and rich soil, certainly in tribute to the brilliance of its statesmen in his day. Upon another occasion Jefferson wrote somewhat bitterly of Delaware's being "held under by force, but always disposed to counter-revolution." One of the classic references to the independence of the State's people.

To me, the history of Delaware has always felt as if it reflected the history of the entire United States of America in miniature. It is indelibly marked by the Native American populations that lived on this land long before recorded history. The Lenni Lenape, the Nanticoke, the Pocomoke-Assateague and Choptank were among the most prominent indigenous tribes who called this beautiful land home. On it they hunted and fished and grew corn, beans and squash, living peacefully except for occasional attacks from the more aggressive Iroquois and Minqua tribes. Storytelling was an integral part of their existence, and the Lenape people inscribed the tales of their long history via paintings and carvings on wooden staffs known as the *Walam Olum*.

Like nearly everywhere in the United States, tragically by the end of the eighteenth century, nearly all the Native peoples of Delaware had been forced by increasing numbers of White European colonists to abandon the lands their ancestors had called home for many thousands of years. Some Native American tribes remain in Delaware today, most notably the Nanticoke Indian Association in the Sussex County town of Millsboro by the Indian River. They operate several historic sites, including the Nanticoke Indian Museum, a National Historic Landmark and the only museum dedicated to the history of Native Americans in the entire state of Delaware. Powwows have been held on two days near the end of September in Millsboro every year since 1977. The Nanticoke Indian Association website says:

The noun Powwow, *from the Narragansett Eastern Algonquian language, is defined as any gathering of Native people. However, in Indian*

Country, we define it as a cultural event that features group singing and dancing by men, women, and children. Through these gatherings, cultural traditions are passed from generation to generation....It is a welcome opportunity to visit with friends and relatives, renew acquaintances, and trade or sell Native arts and crafts including jewelry, pottery, moccasins, ribbon shirts, shawls, dream catchers, and paintings. Above all, Powwows are a time to preserve traditions, to sing to the Creator, and to dance to the heartbeat of the drum.

Although the state of Delaware retains numerous reminders of its indigenous peoples' history through events like this and the names of places, it is heartbreaking to consider all that has been lost to time. One of its most extraordinary relics was known as the Island Field Site, the remains of a Nanticoke village and burial ground dating back to the ninth century located south of the Murderkill River in Kent County that was unearthed in the mid-twentieth century. It was listed in the National Register of Historic Places in 1972 and a museum built where thousands of visitors viewed the exposed human skeletal remains of ancient Native men, women and children. In 1986, members of the Nanticoke tribe protested the desecration of the sacred burial site and the removal of its bones and artifacts for public display. The site was closed to the public soon afterward, and now those buried there can finally rest in peace— or perhaps, not entirely at peace, and with good reason. Stories of paranormal activity in the area surrounding the Island Field Site continue to be reported to this day.

It was, appropriately, on a dark and stormy night in the year 1610 when an English sailor named Samuel Argall found himself and his ship suddenly attacked by nature's violent thunder, horrific lightning and huge ocean waves on his way back from a visit to the colony of Virginia, which had been established just three years earlier in 1607. Fearing death by drowning, Argall and his crew were saved by sailing their ship into a mercifully peaceful body of water that he later named after Lord Thomas De La Warr, who was then the governor of Virginia. That name for the bay, the Delaware, would eventually become the colonial name of the land itself.

The Dutch were the first group of White European colonists who laid claim to the land that would become Delaware. In 1631, they founded the colonial settlement of Swanendael (Valley of the Swans), often modernized by the name Zwaanendael, in what is now known as the town of Lewes, Delaware. The colony consisted of thirty-two people, and all but one were massacred within the first year of the settlement's existence (more on that later). In 1638, the Swedish established colonies they called "New Sweden" throughout the future Delaware landscape. One year later, in 1639, the first known Black person from Africa was brought to the Eastern Shore and enslaved, beginning a shameful legacy that will also be explored further in the following pages.

In 1682, William Penn received a large land grant in the New World from King Charles II that gave him "rights" to the environs subsequently known as Pennsylvania. Because English explorers Henry Hudson and Samuel Argall had "discovered" the waters and land that would become known as Delaware before the Dutch and the Swedes dared settle there, Penn argued he had a claim to those lands as well. Penn won his argument and claimed the "three counties on the Delaware" as his own. It was at this time the three counties were officially named New Castle, Kent and Sussex, as they remain today. It was not until the Declaration of Independence in 1776 that the three counties asserted themselves into one body as the state of Delaware. On December 7, 1787, Delaware ratified the U.S. Constitution, earning its immortal nickname "The First State," much to the chagrin of our proud neighbor Pennsylvania, the cradle of the American Revolution, which was admitted to the new union on December 12, 1787, as the *second* state, five days after Delaware made its indelible mark on American history.

And as far as ghost stories and legends go, the historic state of Delaware has them all. Not only are there numerous tales of haunted houses, bridges, historic sites and cemeteries, but if you dig deep enough, you will also find chilling stories of demonic dogs, voodoo, vanishing hitchhikers, alien encounters, serial killers, swamp monsters and other cryptids, pirates, shipwrecks, buried treasure, ghost ships, phantom lights and an evil entity known as the Bad Weather Witch. Unlike the more famous town of Sleepy Hollow, the state of Delaware has a real Headless Horseman. I wish I could include all these tales in the book, but I have narrowed it down to my favorites, the ones that creep me out the most. These eerie pieces of folklore have been handed down for generations, and by reading this book, you are helping keep these priceless old yarns alive for the future. A good story never truly dies.

So, settle down now and turn the lights down low. Read these terrifying tales and then tell them to others around your own campfire or in your home on a suitably dark and stormy night. When I sat down to begin writing this book, the moment I started typing, a light by my bed suddenly fell to the floor with a loud crash. That was not the only unexplained occurrence that happened to me while I was working on this project. I took it as a sign the ghosts of Delaware were watching me, and I hope they approve of how I have told their stories. And perhaps, as you read this late at night and your eyes grow heavy, you, too, may get the eerie feeling that you are not alone, that something might be lurking in the shadows right outside your bedroom door.

Happy reading, and pleasant dreams.

1
PHANTOMS AT FORT DELAWARE

The state of Delaware is filled with many ghostly echoes of its past history, but perhaps the most famous and the most haunted location of them all is Fort Delaware, located on Pea Patch Island approximately one mile from the mainland of Delaware City in New Castle County. Virtually every paranormal television series has visited the fort at one time or another, and those who investigate this historic site almost always have encounters there that would cause most people to run away screaming into the night. So, it is fitting that we begin our tour of haunted Delaware here. It is also the location where I myself saw a ghost for the first time in my life.

In 1938, the Federal Writers' Project of the Works Progress Administration combed the state of Delaware to create an exhaustive study of its history and folklore, including its tales of ghosts and hauntings. The resulting book, *Delaware: A Guide to the First State*, is long out of print, but I believe it is the best book ever written about the place I grew up in. In these pages, I will quote from it frequently, and I encourage everyone to find a copy for themselves. It contains vivid descriptions of Delaware's people and places that would likely have been lost to time otherwise. The book describes Fort Delaware as it was in the first decades of the twentieth century:

> On a marshy island in midstream, is the grim and bleak gray mass of Fort Delaware, a huge granite pentagon commanding a southward sweep of river and bay. Tiers of empty gun ports look out from casements in the walls and jutting bastions above an encircling moat filled with dark water. On the

earth-covered upper battlements trees have grown fantastically, their roots twining with dungeon ventilators, their branches twisted by gales. Only the flag and the Monday wash of a non-commissioned officer's wife flutter gaily in the breeze to relieve the sullen melancholy of the great old fortress. The silence is usually heavy and unbroken.

A dark and shadowy Civil War fortress surrounded by a moat on an isolated island where thousands of Confederate prisoners died—what better place could you expect to find ghosts from the past with unfinished business? For many children educated in Delaware public schools (East Millsboro Elementary School for me), a field trip to Fort Delaware was mandatory. I first visited the fort on a class trip when I was in the fifth grade. To get to it, you must take a ferry from Delaware City over the Delaware River. There is no other way. Once you land on Pea Patch Island, you walk along an extended wooden boardwalk and then ride a jitney through thick marshland for several minutes before arriving at the fort itself. Then, with the imposing structure of Fort Delaware before you, you cross the moat and walk inside.

Fort Delaware was declared a state park in 1951, and ever since it has operated as a living history site, where staff members dress and talk to visitors as if it is still 1864. If you want to ask the staff a contemporary question, you are told at the beginning of your visit to ask them to "take off their hat." Only then will they break character and respond to you in a modern way.

On my fifth-grade field trip, I was enraptured by the history all around me at Fort Delaware. With the other students in my class, we were touring what is known as the "dungeons," small cells where Confederate prisoners were held and sometimes chained to the walls. I suddenly realized that I had lost my class and I was all alone. I was afraid of getting in trouble for not staying with the group, and I was also scared because I had no idea how to get out. Then, a little farther down the hallway, I heard voices talking. Thinking that was where my teacher and classmates had gone, I followed the voices.

The voices I heard led me to one of the cells in the dungeons. The door to the cell was closed, but there was a small window with prison bars, covered by cobwebs. I looked through that barred window, and I saw two men sitting in the prison cell at an old wooden table opposite each other. One of the men wore a crisp, nearly new, blue Union army uniform. He had a long brown beard and blue eyes. Across from him sat a thin, pale man dressed in what remained of his once glorious gray Confederate army uniform, but now it was nothing but rags. The man in the Union uniform turned his head from the Confederate soldier he had been speaking to and looked at me; he

Fort Delaware on Pea Patch Island in 1998. *U.S. Army Corps of Engineers.*

looked directly into my eyes. I got the feeling that I was not supposed to be there, that I was interrupting something I shouldn't see.

I assumed I had interrupted a rehearsal for the reenactors of Fort Delaware, so I quickly walked away, out of the dungeons and into the bright light of the parade ground. I found my classmates and was relieved no one had noticed I was missing.

Our next stop on the tour was the officers' quarters, and after the reenactor had explained the rooms and my classmates and chaperones drifted out of the door, I asked him to take off his hat. He did. Then I asked him about the two reenactors I had seen in the dungeons. He got very pale and said there were no staff members ever stationed in the dungeons. More than that, all the cell doors were rusted shut. No one could get into those rooms.

No one alive, anyway.

I realized, in that moment at Fort Delaware in the fifth grade, that I had seen a ghost.

About two years later, I went with my family on a ghost tour of Fort Delaware led by master storyteller and author Ed Okonowicz. He was collecting stories for his upcoming book *Civil War Ghosts at Fort Delaware*, which remains definitive. At the encouragement of my mother, as we traveled over the water in the dark, I told Mr. Okonowicz what had happened to me. He listened to my story very kindly as we traveled to Fort Delaware on Halloween eve.

My story didn't make it into his book. I never dreamed I'd finally be able to tell it in my own.

———————◆———————

THE WRITERS OF *DELAWARE: A Guide to the First State* recorded, "The legend of Pea Patch Island is that a vessel loaded with peas foundered on a bar in the river, the peas sprouted, catching floating debris, and little by little the island was formed. Testimony that 'in 1773 the island was only the size of a man's hat' appears in the record of a suit brought by the state of Delaware in 1839."

In its early history, Pea Patch Island is also referred to as Pip Ash Island by Major Pierre L'Enfant. He was a military engineer chiefly remembered by history as the man who designed the original layout of Washington, D.C., and on May 16, 1794 Pierre L'Enfant wrote a letter to the secretary of war that would significantly alter the course of the little island's destiny:

> *I recommend a fort on Pip Ash, and batteries at New Castle should be provided for; not because of its great commercial interest, but because of its importance when militarily viewed....This situation—New Castle— is most happily circumstanced to be made strong and to unite all that is requisite—a grand garrison....Upon the Pip Ash Island, it cannot be questioned but that the pass may be well armed, and that proper works erected there would protect the whole river bank.*

Despite Pierre L'Enfant's enthusiastic recommendation, it would take many years until his order to construct a fort on Pea Patch Island was finally completed. Some might even say that efforts to build on the island were cursed, with the land itself doing everything it could to reject human habitation.

In 1813, the first official order to begin work on a fort at Pea Patch Island was given. Work did not commence on the island until Christmas Day 1814, and it proceeded extremely slowly. Most of the island was approximately four feet above sea level, and its highest ground was only ten feet above

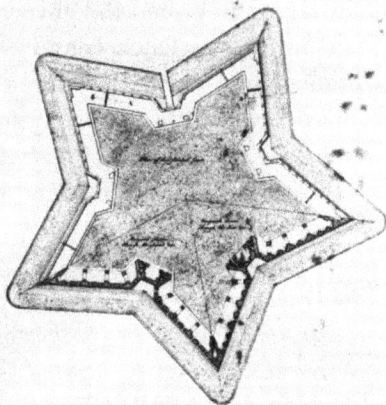

Sketch of the Star Fort
version of Fort Delaware.
U.S. Army Corps of Engineers.

sea level, which left Pea Patch prone to completely flooding if tides in the Delaware River were even slightly higher than normal. Because of this, it was necessary to alter the structure of the island to prevent flooding, which was a complex and expensive endeavor. The structure, nicknamed the Star Fort due to the shape of its design, began to be take shape in 1820. Almost immediately after the building began, workers and officers stationed on Pea Patch Island began to fall ill with mysterious respiratory infections in large numbers. Then it became clear that the structure built so far was shifting with the tides, cracking, sinking into the perpetually muddy earth.

The winter of 1831 was an especially unforgiving one for those living on Pea Patch Island. The Delaware River was close to completely freezing over, leaving those at the Star Fort cut off from the mainland. Many of the inhabitants became sick, and some died, their decaying remains lying out in cold houses, unable to be buried in the frozen earth. Then on February 9, 1831, the Star Fort caught on fire. No source for the blaze was ever discovered, but it decimated the wooden structure, leaving only charred stones. The military was forced to abandon the ruins of the fort on Pea Patch Island on February 10, 1831, leaving no living inhabitants.

Two years later, in 1833, the United States was ready to try again. It was declared that a new structure made of stone and brick should be built on Pea Patch Island and that its name would be Fort Delaware. After the military decided to start building from scratch, it was discovered that deep under the layers of mud and sand on Pea Patch Island there was rock, so it was decided to construct a stone fort on pilings driven deep into the earth. Although time consuming, it was thought that this would finally allow a stable structure to exist on the island. However, in 1838, a man named James Humphrey sued the government, asserting that he had a claim of ownership to Pea Patch Island. This caused all work on Fort Delaware to immediately cease, and for a full decade the island sat completely abandoned while the case went through the court system.

In their excellent book *Unlikely Allies: Fort Delaware's Prison Community in the Civil War*, authors Dale Fetzer and Bruce Mowday write of this unlucky time in the fort's history:

> *In the ten years since the army vacated Pea Patch, nature had not been kind to the island. In 1839 an unusually high tide completely flooded the island....Some of the material, especially the timbers, was washed away. Again, in October 1846 a high tide flooded the island. In fact, the oldest inhabitants of the region claimed that the 1846 tide was the highest in memory....Pea Patch Island had become a tangled wasteland. Debris was scattered everywhere, vegetation had grown over the brick and stone piles, the engines were relics, and most of the timbers were gone.*

Finally, in 1848 Pea Patch Island was back within the government's control. Throughout the 1850s, the military worked on building the five-sided Fort Delaware visitors can see on the island today. The builders worked ten hours a day, six days a week, and were forbidden to leave the island for the duration. More than three hundred people lived on Pea Patch during this time, the most human beings the island had ever seen up to that point in its history. Fort Delaware would have the luxury of indoor plumbing and even flushable toilets, which emptied out into the moat surrounding the fort and then periodically flushed out into the Delaware River. The system did not always work, leaving the fort surrounded by water fouled by human waste.

This period of Fort Delaware's construction was overseen by Major John Sanders. After ten years of seemingly unending work, he declared that the fort, although not completed, would be ready for military service in 1858. Sadly, Major Sanders would not live to see the fruits of his labor. He died on July 29, 1858, becoming another sad addition to the list of people who died on Pea Patch Island for the sake of Fort Delaware. On the day Major John Sanders died, to honor his memory, the community paused all work and fell into respectful silence.

Fetzer and Mowday write in *Unlikely Allies*:

Fort Delaware was a marvel of military engineering.... The determination of the government—as seen through the actions of several secretaries of war, including the likes of James Monroe and Jefferson Davis—to conclude the project was as remarkable as the project itself. This American Goliath boasted indoor plumbing, modern defensive architecture, innovative gunnery platforms, and the capability to hold a waterborne enemy at bay for months. Fort Delaware was truly the locked door to the seaport of Philadelphia.

Construction on Fort Delaware would not officially be completed until 1868, but it became an integral part of history during the American Civil War of 1861–65, a time of horrific pain and bloodshed that left numerous ghostly echoes within Fort Delaware's stone walls. Its state-of-the-art guns would never be fired in battle with the enemy, but the fort would become notorious as a prison for captured Confederate soldiers, many of whom it seems have never left the island.

Disease remained a constant specter on Pea Patch Island. The first recorded death of a prisoner at Fort Delaware was on April 9, 1862. Captain Lewis Holloway, twenty-one years old, caught pneumonia and did not survive. Outside of the fort itself, long wooden barracks were constructed to house the prisoners of war. They were stifling hot during the summer and freezing cold in the winter, despite the presence of a pot-bellied stove. Private George M. Green wrote in a letter home that the Confederate prisoners "get so sassy sometimes that we put them in the dungeons and feed them on bread and water until they get tame."

These "dungeons" were really the casemates and powder magazines, and they remain nightmare fuel now just as they did for Confederate prisoners during the Civil War. They are cavernous brick structures with only small windows to let in light. Here, prisoners were sometimes chained or placed

A view of the casemates or "dungeons" at Fort Delaware.

in solitary confinement. Names of past prisoners are still discernable carved into the brick, grim reminders of past torture. Union soldiers who deserted their posts at Fort Delaware were routinely captured and then had their skin shamefully branded with the letter *D* for deserter. Fetzer and Mowday also describe how

> *a miscreant could be "bucked and gagged," which involved the use of a long pole placed in the crook of the elbow, with the prisoner's hands tied in front of him, and a stick or bayonet, secured by a leather thong, in the mouth. At Fort Delaware, those who were bucked and gagged were then hoisted by rope to the ceiling of the sally port, where they were suspended for the duration of the punishment.*

The night of July 15, 1862, was a dark and stormy one. During the torrential downpour and ferocious winds, nineteen prisoners escaped from Fort Delaware by swimming across the river from Pea Patch Island to the mainland of Delaware City. None of them was recaptured. Some may have made it to the shore and been helped south by Confederate sympathizers. It is certain that some of them drowned in the river during the storm. Over the course of the Civil War, many prisoners would attempt to escape, some even getting to the river by going through the sewage system in desperation. How many men drowned trying to escape the island is unknown, but it explains why sometimes people traveling to or from Fort Delaware by boat have been terrified to see human hands emerging from the dark river as if pleading for help that never came.

The Battle of Gettysburg in July 1863 changed life on Pea Patch Island forever. After that bloody battle, which helped turn the tide of the Civil War, there were 12,595 Confederate prisoners at the fort, and the total population of the island reached an all-time high of over 16,000 souls. This was more people than lived in the city of Wilmington, so, for a time, Fort Delaware on Pea Patch Island became the largest, most populated "city" in the First State.

By the end of July 1863, 111 Confederate prisoners had died, and the island's population continued to be ravaged by disease, especially smallpox. Some prisoners were exchanged or released, but there were still far too many for the fort to accommodate. Private Joseph E. Purvis, a Confederate prisoner from the Battle of Gettysburg, could likely have spoken for all the prisoners of war as he wrote in his diary: "I'm still confined in this wretched place. God grant they may send us away very soon, for this is the last place

Confederate prisoners arriving at Fort Delaware. *Delaware Public Archives.*

on earth to me." As summer turned to fall and the weather grew colder and colder, Purvis wrote: "Sickness increases every day I believe and so does wickedness. I never saw the like in my life before and I hope I never do again….Eight or nine of us die every night."

In September 1863, the death toll at Fort Delaware had risen to 327, mostly due to the smallpox epidemic. Those who went into the island's hospital almost never left it alive. From the Battle of Gettysburg in July to December 1863, 1,222 Confederate prisoners died—almost exactly half of the deaths at Fort Delaware took place within this period. It soon became apparent that Pea Patch Island was not able to hold its dead. Because of the frequent high tides and muddy soil, decomposing bodies would eventually come back up to the surface. Corpses were placed in simple wooden coffins and then traveled on what became known as the Death Boat to be interred in mass graves at a cemetery in Finn's Point, New Jersey. One Confederate prisoner escaped from Fort Delaware by removing a corpse from its coffin, taking the dead body's place in the coffin for the boat ride to Finn's Point and then jumping out of the coffin once it reached the cemetery and running away, probably scaring the gravediggers almost to death.

Visiting Fort Delaware in July 1863, infamous Philadelphia surgeon Dr. Silas Weir Mitchell called Pea Patch Island "an inferno of detained rebels…a thousand ill; twelve thousand on an island which should hold four…the living have more life *on* them than *in* them." There are stories handed down, perhaps apocryphal, that Union guards would sometimes throw live rats into the barracks to enjoy watching the starved Confederate prisoners fight over a warm meal.

In 1864, conditions for the prisoners at Fort Delaware worsened. This was partially due to an order given by General Albin Schoepf intended to enforce discipline among the prisoners. In effect, it gave the Union guards a

Top: Re-created exterior of one of the prisoners' barracks constructed at Fort Delaware.

Bottom: Pittsburgh Heavy Artillery soldiers at Fort Delaware in 1864. *John L. Gihon.*

license to kill: "Should the prisoner fail to halt when so ordered, the sentinel must enforce his orders by bayonet or ball." According to some historical records, at least twelve Confederate prisoners were shot and killed at Fort Delaware because of this order, some accidentally and some on purpose. There may well have been more.

When the Civil War finally came to an end in 1865, approximately 32,000 men had been imprisoned at Fort Delaware. Of those 32,000 prisoners, 2,460 of them never left Pea Patch Island alive. The last prisoner to die at Fort Delaware was a nineteen-year-old named Thomas Jowers, who succumbed to illness on July 30, 1865. In the early decades of the twentieth century, Fort Delaware was slowly abandoned, and vandals stripped the buildings of its wooden furniture and doors. The prisoners' barracks, the hospital, the chapel and all other buildings except the stone fort itself eventually vanished, leaving the spirits of the dead all alone on Pea Patch Island. But they would not be silent for long.

EVER SINCE FORT DELAWARE State Park opened to the public in 1951, both visitors and the reenactors who work there have experienced paranormal activity on Pea Patch Island. Unlike many historic sites, Fort Delaware has embraced the spooky side of its history, hosting ghost tours and paranormal investigations at the fort annually during the month of October. One reason why the haunting of Pea Patch Island remains so strong is perhaps because it is operated as a living history site. The officers' quarters, the kitchen, the mess halls and the prisoners' barracks have all been painstakingly restored to look as they would have in the year 1864, when Fort Delaware was deep in the maelstrom of the Civil War. Perhaps because so much is as it was during those years, the ghosts still feel very much at home on Pea Patch Island.

As soon as you cross the drawbridge over the moat and enter Fort Delaware via the sally port (the only way in and the only way out), you may feel that you are being watched. This location is said to be haunted by the specter of a Union soldier, Private Stefano, who immigrated to the United States from Italy. Private Stefano was given the task of looking after the high-ranking Confederate officers who were kept prisoner in rooms above the sally port so they would not be able to mingle with or influence the Rebel soldiers they had once commanded. Day after day, Private Stefano walked the slippery stone steps up to the area where the Confederate officers were held. On one fateful day, Private Stefano lost his footing and fell. He landed hard on the granite floor of the sally port, cracking his skull open, his blood spreading over the gray stone as he died. To this day, visitors newly arrived at Fort Delaware have reported seeing the apparition of a soldier walk past them and then vanish or feeling touched

A view of the front and only entrance into the fort. You cross the moat and enter the darkness of the sally port.

A strange
hallway
upstairs.

by a phantom hand as they listen to the reenactor's introductory speech. Some more sensitive folks have sworn they have seen fresh red bloodstains appear on the old gray stones by the stairs.

The rooms above the sally port where Confederate officers were imprisoned are not open to the public. But they are sometimes made available to Civil War reenactors who visit Fort Delaware. In his essential book *Civil War Ghosts at Fort Delaware*, Ed Okonowicz relates a chilling tale told to him by a reenactor named Bob Steves:

> *One day, Bob arrived to work at the fort, walked up to the second floor—where the Rebel officers had lived—and entered a room that was used as a dressing area. While he was putting on his uniform, Bob noticed another reenactor, who apparently had arrived earlier and was already dressed. The stranger walked by Bob's doorway and headed down the narrow hall. Instinctively, Bob called out a greeting and went into the hall....The hallway was empty. There was no one there.*

As you walk the grounds of Fort Delaware, you feel as if you are in another time. In this way, it is a perfect place for ghost stories. You may stumble upon the chance to watch and hear one of the island's guns fired toward Delaware City. You may find Union soldiers demonstrating how they fired their rifles on the green grass of the parade ground inside the fort. You might wander through the dungeons and feel afraid. You may stumble upon the commander's office and finally find yourself in Fort Delaware's laundry room, pharmacy or one of its kitchens, in which a reenactor cooks you spiced apples the old-fashioned way, over a stove fueled by fire.

Ed Okonowicz interviewed a kitchen reenactor named Linda Jennings for *Civil War Ghosts at Fort Delaware*, and what she said has become part of this island's haunting legend. While working in the kitchen in 2005, Linda saw the apparition of a Black woman suddenly appear:

I looked over in the corner and I saw a lady staring at us. I did a double take and kind of nodded. Because there were children with me, I didn't say anything. Her apron was filthy, cruddy. It was singed at the bottom, probably from working in the kitchen. She walked around, came close and examined what we were cooking. She was looking in the pots. She vanished for a short time and then came back. She looked at me. I felt like she was nodding approval at what we were doing. Then she turned around and walked into a wall. And that's when everybody got the clue that this was not just part of the cast....I think they are here because we are here. They can be here all the time, and we just don't see them.

The area where the kitchen ghost disappeared also has a cold spot that cannot be explained, especially when the fire is burning in the kitchen stove and the room is stifling hot. There is a pantry next to the cold spot in the kitchen that has also been the site of paranormal activity, including the sound of a woman's voice being heard when no one else is nearby.

Linda's husband, Lee Jennings, has also experienced unsettling things while working at Fort Delaware over the years, particularly in the dungeons, which seem to be the most haunted areas of Pea Patch Island. Ghosts have been experienced in the dungeons by visitors and staff countless times over the decades. Lee Jennings related in *Civil War Ghosts at Fort Delaware*:

It's hard when you're working in a dark place by yourself to not be disconcerted by the sound of somebody behind you that you can't see. I have heard footsteps, I've heard hushed conversations, but most of the time it's

The haunted kitchen.

33

just this presence here. It's like you're being followed. I recall when we first started our work here, walking through the dungeon areas was unpleasant. It was not a nice place to be. You would start out walking, and you end up running to get out.

As the sun sets and the tourists go home, the staff does a thorough search of the island to make sure everyone has gone. Once they do, the reenactors are finally able to take the *Delafort* ferry back to the mainland and the modern world. It is then that the many phantoms at Fort Delaware have the place all to themselves. At night, when the island is empty, many witnesses on boats passing by Pea Patch Island have noticed a light where no light should be. Up on the ramparts on the New Jersey side of Fort Delaware, the apparition of a man in a black cloak has been seen carrying a lantern. This eerie moving light on top of the fort has been seen by dozens of people over the years, including author and historian Ed Okonowicz himself. Some who have gotten a closer view of this apparition have sworn it also appears to be headless.

The ghosts of Fort Delaware, it seems, are still guarding this old historic landmark. Perhaps the unearthly light on the ramparts at night is a warning to the living to stay away—or perhaps it is an invitation, a dare to come closer and find out just what is lurking within the dark chambers of this haunted, and haunting, relic of the American Civil War's bloody atrocities.

2
ROCKWOOD MANSION REVENANTS

graduate student named Gilbert Tapley Vincent wrote a thoroughly researched master's thesis for the University of Delaware in 1972 that was republished in 1998 as *Romantic Rockwood: A Rural Gothic Villa Near Wilmington, Delaware*. His evocative opening paragraph describes the eternal allure of the Rockwood Mansion and estate like this:

> *The outstanding significance of Rockwood lies not in its individual details or objects, nor even in its architecture, but in its remarkable portrayal of an age. Constructed between the years 1851 and 1857, the estate comprised a mansion house, porter's lodge, stable, carriage house, gardener's cottage, and 211 acres. As it exists today, it is an unusually complete and effective statement of early Victorian taste…that is fast vanishing from the American scene.*

To walk the grounds and enter the mansion of Rockwood today is to be transported into another age, a vision of a long-vanished Victorian past that remains startlingly present—because the exquisite mansion of Rockwood, and the landscape surrounding it, have long been known as one of the most haunted locations in the state of Delaware. Rockwood has been featured on *Ghost Hunters* and many other prominent paranormal television programs. It well earns its reputation as a hotbed of a well-documented supernatural activity, as well as a historical gem that offers its many visitors a trip back in time to a world of nineteenth-century elegance.

The Rockwood Mansion in 2010. *Photograph by SmallBones, public domain.*

Rockwood was built by a man named Joseph Shipley. Born on December 4, 1795, in the city of Wilmington, Delaware, Shipley spent a great deal of his adult life in Liverpool, England. Once he moved there in 1819, Joseph quickly distanced himself from the austere Quaker faith he had been raised in, writing in a letter to a friend that he had purchased "a best super Blue cloth Coat with Velvet Collar and Gold Gilt cuffs" and attended a fancy-dress party, a scandalous fact that somehow made its way back to his devoutly religious family in Wilmington. Joseph Shipley became a merchant banker in England, and over the years, he amassed a large fortune.

In 1846, Joseph Shipley built his own English country house named Wyncote, designed by architect George Williams. However, by 1850 Joseph Shipley's health had begun to decline. He had been plagued by attacks of gout for over a decade, and now he was forced to slow down. Shipley made the decision to leave Liverpool and retire near the city of Wilmington, where he was born. On a visit home to Delaware in 1847, Joseph was taking a country walk with his nephew Edward Bringhurst, and Shipley suddenly remarked, "Edward, this is my idea of a situation for a country place. If thee can arrange to buy it, I would come here to live."

Joseph Shipley was standing on the exact spot where the Rockwood Mansion would eventually be constructed between 1851 and 1854. Like

Joseph Shipley, the man who built Rockwood. *From the Shipley-Bringhurst-Hargraves Collection, Morris Library, University of Delaware, 181 South College Avenue, Newark, Delaware 19717.*

his beloved Wyncote, Shipley had Rockwood and its surrounding landscape designed by George Williams. The estate received its name from the fact that the grounds were strewn with large granite boulders, some of which may have been used to construct the mansion's gray stone exterior. Most of the materials used to build Rockwood were local; however, Joseph Shipley did choose to import the cast iron and plate glass from England. The final product of the house and grounds was, and remains, breathtaking. Rockwood's impressive rural Gothic architecture was the first of its kind in Delaware.

Joseph Shipley moved into his grand estate at Rockwood in 1854, bringing the entirety of the Wyncote household with him. This included his favorite dogs, Toby and Branker, as well as Scottish gardener Robert Salisbury and housekeeper Audrey Douglas. Shipley never married or had any children and was often infirm during his final years, having to be wheeled about the house and gardens in his "invalid chair." Joseph Shipley died at Rockwood on May 9, 1867, at the age of seventy-two. He willed the estate to his sisters for their lifetimes, with the stipulation that after his youngest sister died, the estate would go up for auction. Hannah Shipley died in 1891. The auction of Rockwood was won by Joseph Shipley's niece Sarah Shipley Bringhurst in 1892. Sarah then gifted the estate to her son, Edward Bringhurst Jr.

The great-nephew of Joseph Shipley, Edward Bringhurst Jr. and his wife, Anna Webb Bringhurst, had four children. The eldest child, Elizabeth, nicknamed Bessie, was already married and living in an Irish castle called Kilwaughter at the time her parents purchased Rockwood, but she returned to help decorate the new family mansion with the latest exquisite Victorian furnishings and decorations as well as adding ten rooms to the servants' wing in 1895. Elizabeth "Bessie" Bringhurst Galt-Smith hobnobbed in the circles of high society all over the world, finally moving into Rockwood itself in 1923 for the final years of her life.

The other Bringhurst offspring who moved into the grand house in 1892 were Mary, Edith and little Edward III. This was, for a time, the golden age of Rockwood, when its fifty-room mansion and lusciously landscaped grounds were filled with the joyous tumult of family life. Together with their staff of hardworking servants—including maids, housekeepers, cooks, a butler, laundry workers and gardeners—the Bringhurst clan lived a life of comfortable luxury that in many ways resembled a real-life American version of *Downton Abbey*.

The patriarch of the family, Edward Bringhurst Jr., died in 1912 at the age of seventy-seven after living at Rockwood for exactly two decades. His wife, Anna Bringhurst, lived for eleven years after her husband died, passing on herself in 1923 at the age of eighty. After their parents' deaths, sisters Bessie and Mary often had lavish dinner parties at Rockwood. But only nine years later, in 1932, Elizabeth "Bessie" Bringhurst Galt-Smith became the fourth person to die inside the walls of the stately mansion. She was sixty-nine years old at the time of her death.

The ruins of "Edward's Playhouse" on the grounds of Rockwood.

Little Edward Bringhurst III was only eight years old when his family moved into Rockwood, filling the house and grounds with the laughter and play of a child for the first time. A small building on the grounds was set up as a playroom for him, and the ruins of that structure are still visible today and known as "Edward's Playhouse." As Edward III grew into adulthood, he is never known to have dated women and he never married. However, he did possess a love of fine furniture and antiques as well as being an amateur photographer and aviation enthusiast. In 1911, at the age of twenty-seven, Edward III was presented to King George V of England. After this incident, he legally changed his name to Edward Bringhurst V, some say because he believed he was on the same social level as the current king of England.

Eventually, Edward Bringhurst V contracted tuberculosis and spent many years in and out of sanitoriums in an effort to cure the deadly disease. Edward's health, made worse by an aviation accident, continued to decline until he died in the Delaware Hospital a few miles from the Rockwood estate in 1939. He was only fifty-five years old at the time of his death.

Now, Edith and Mary were the only Bringhursts left. Edith married a man named Alexander Sellers at Rockwood in 1897, but then they made their home in Radnor, Pennsylvania. Edith was the only Bringhurst sibling to have children, one of whom, Nancy, would eventually inherit Rockwood many years later. Edith Bringhurst Sellers died in 1947 at the age of seventy-three, leaving her sister Mary Bringhurst in the grand house all alone, tended by her faithful servants.

Like original owner Joseph Shipley and her little brother, Edward III/V, Mary Bringhurst never married or had children, and there is no evidence in the surviving historical record that she ever had any male suitors during her lifetime. She was regarded as a kind and a caring woman who loved the theater and could play the piano and the banjo beautifully. Born in 1865 at the end of the Civil War, Mary Bringhurst died in the Rockwood Mansion at the age of one hundred, in 1965, at the height of the civil rights movement—an extraordinary witness to American history.

According to housekeeper Edna Blunt, after Mary, now completely blind, had to be moved to a downstairs room, "She laid there for five years and didn't know anybody or anything." However, near the end of her full century of life, Mary Bringhurst made clear to her niece, Nancy, of her "primary desire to preserve the beauty of Rockwood."

After Mary Bringhurst's death in 1965, Rockwood was inherited by her beloved niece, Nancy Bringhurst Sellers Hargraves. Upon Nancy's death in 1972, with no more family descendants to inherit the property for the first time in Rockwood's history, she willed the estate to an as yet unnamed nonprofit organization "for the enjoyment of present and future generations." It was just as her aunt, Mary Bringhurst, had wished before she died.

In 1973, the Rockwood Mansion and its surrounding landscape were acquired by New Castle County, with the organization Friends of Rockwood as its caretakers. The property was added to the National Register of Historic Places in 1976, and ever since, Rockwood Museum and Park has been open for the public to enjoy. However, it has become apparent that many of the people who lived at Rockwood between 1854 and 1972 have never left the house and grounds.

In a chapter of his 1995 book *Welcome Inn*, Ed Okonowicz interviewed a woman named Suzie who had been a volunteer guide at Rockwood since it opened to the public. Suzie recalled speaking with the housekeeper of the mansion's final owner, Nancy Sellers Hargraves, who related that after one night of terror, Mrs. Hargraves never spent another night in the house alone:

> *According to her housekeeper…Mrs. Hargraves was alone one night, when her husband was away. She later said she heard all kinds of things, all night long, walking around. Mrs. Hargraves locked herself in her bedroom and pushed chairs up against the door and wouldn't come out.*

Edna, a former housekeeper at Rockwood, recorded her own testimony in 1984 about a frightening haunting that occurred during the time Mrs. Hargraves lived in the house. She said:

> *One year, Mrs. Hargraves had brought this cook from Maine. Her name was Florence. Every morning I went in Florence would say, "I didn't sleep last night. Something bothers me back there." I said, "Well, what is it?" She said, "I don't know. It gets over my head and I can hear this heavy breathing. I can't sleep."…It was like somebody gasping for breath…. Sister Mary was raised there [at Rockwood] and she was a hundred years old when she died….Well, Margaret, had worked for her for thirty-six years as a cook. She had an apartment on the third floor and Margaret married John. They were all brought from Ireland by sister Bessie. They would go over and bring back cheap help, you know, and then they would work out their passage. Well, after Margaret came over John came. John*

worked in the yard or whatever and after a while they got married. They bought a house in Gordy Estates. Margaret said John went home that day to cut the grass so he wouldn't have to do it on the weekend....It was their weekend off. And when he came back it was so hot, he said he was going to go upstairs [to the apartment] *and lie down for a while. So, when* [Margaret] *finished work and went up to tell him they were ready to go home, she found him dead. And I don't know if that was John....But that's what we think it was, him gasping for breath back there.*

Staff and volunteers at Rockwood Park and Museum have continued to experience paranormal activity into the present day. If anything, the numerous ghosts of the mansion seem to be getting even bolder with the passage of time. Former director of Rockwood Philip (now retired) wrote of the house's haunting reputation:

Since my arrival here at Rockwood two years ago I have been fascinated by, and somewhat skeptical of, the "ghosts" that inhabit the Mansion. There is a long list of strange noises, sightings of unusual "things," stories of tragedy in the House, and people claiming to have hair stand up on the back of their necks, claiming there was a "presence" near them. A long-time servant claims there is a secret room in the basement. I have looked but have not found it... yet. Some current employees will not go to the second floor at night.

It wasn't long before Philip had his own paranormal experience inside Rockwood Mansion. On October 29, 2011, he appeared on an episode of the television series *My Ghost Story*, where he related this tale:

One time, I was closing the place up, and I go into every room to find out if everything is locked up. We have a tearoom, and there's no doorway, there's curtains. I looked to my left and sitting in one of the chairs in the tearoom was this person. I thought that the staff hadn't asked him to leave. And so, I looked, and I stared at him, and he looked at me. He didn't move. I suddenly got all chills all over me, and I—I turned away and I said, "I SEE YOU." And I turned back, and he was gone. That was the first time I'd actually saw a real full, in flesh, apparition. So, I went downstairs, and the ladies looked at me and they said, "You saw a ghost, didn't you?" I knew it was Edward [Bringhurst Jr.] *and it totally unnerved me. I can guarantee you...it was not a figment of my imagination.*

Rick and Alice have done much to document the haunted history of Rockwood in recent years, and both of them were gracious enough to provide me with many records of the unexplained phenomena inside the mansion and on the grounds that they have collected. Alice wrote a room-by-room assessment of the ghostly goings on. Here are some highlights:

THE UPSTAIRS HALL: Someone visiting the Bringhursts heard a tapping noise in the upper hall, sounding like a cane on the floor. As the guest looked toward the sound, he saw an elderly woman walking along the upper hall with a cane.... The visitor assumed that she was another guest he had not yet met. When the mystery lady did not show up for dinner, however, the guest questioned the Bringhursts, who assured him that all their guests were present. After dinner, the family brought out photo albums to see if the witness could identify the mystery lady. She was indeed recognized as a long-dead relative who walked with a cane.

THE ANTEROOM: Rose, past president of the Friends of Rockwood and a former guide, related this creepy tale. She was giving a tour one Saturday to a group of five people. She walked completely into the anteroom.... As she talked about the room and furnishings, she felt a little nudge on her shoulder. She found one of the bookcase doors had drifted open, so she closed it carefully and tightly. Before she left the anteroom, it happened again! She jokingly told her group that one of the ghosts must want the door open, and she wasn't about to argue with a Rockwood ghost. Rose and her group proceeded to the dining room.... When it was time to proceed upstairs, she peeked into the anteroom one more time and found the bookcase door completely closed!

THE SERVANTS' BEDROOM: Several years ago, Jack, the previous director, discovered that he was having serious water damage due to an overflowing tub in the long-disused servants' bathroom on the third floor. When he investigated, he found the tub full to overflowing, but the faucets were not on. He made sure that all sources of water to the tub were completely turned off. Within days, it happened again! This time, Jack had all the water pipes removed.

THE SERVANTS' STAIRCASE: Many guides and many visitors have heard the sounds of swishing skirts on the servants' staircase. It seems to be loud enough to cause people to turn their heads and look up the stairs, expecting to see someone coming down. I witnessed this on a tour when several ladies on my tour heard the same thing and all looked up the staircase at the same time.

THE WINTER GARDEN: Several years ago, a guide greeted two ladies at the door. One lady said she had come to Rockwood before, but this time she wanted to bring her friend....Her friend made her living as a psychic.... The psychic said that she saw a well-dressed gentleman in a wheelchair in the winter garden, and that he seemed lost and confused. The guide said that it must be Mr. Shipley, and he's confused because...that room didn't exist before 1913. [Joseph Shipley died in 1867.]

ROAD TO UPPER PARKING: While I was on duty in the dining room, I was pointing out the portraits of family members to a woman....When the woman saw Sarah Shipley Bringhurst in the portrait with Edward III, she really did a double take. She told me she just saw this woman....The visitor had parked her car...and started to take her afternoon walk on the old road that leads to the upper parking lot. She walked past a woman walking her dog. She said hello, but the woman looked at her without speaking. She took

A ghostly woman in white and a phantom dog in the window? *The Rockwood Paranormal Experience Team.*

special notice of her because the woman looked very plain and severe and was wearing a long black cape. This struck her as odd because it was a very warm afternoon. After she passed the woman, she turned around to take another look. There was no one there....This woman insisted that Sarah Shipley Bringhurst was the woman she saw.

MARY BRINGHURST'S BEDROOM: Almost every time I close Mary Bringhurst's door, it sticks, and I have a great deal of trouble opening it to let my group continue the tour. I can't see WHY it sticks. There is light showing all around the door and the knob turns easily....I say, "Miss Mary, these visitors are enjoying your lovely home, and I would really like to show them the rest of Rockwood." I find then that the door opens easily and effortlessly.

There are not only human spirits haunting Rockwood—there are canine ghosts as well. Over the years, both the Shipley and Bringhurst families kept at least forty named dogs as pets. On a patch of lawn shaded by trees near the mansion's conservatory there was once an extensive pet cemetery, its markers now gone, eroded by time. There are two mentions of a phantom dog recorded in the anecdotes collected by Rick and other museum docents:

Saturday, October 18, 2014: Rick and Alice were on a ghost tour....On the second floor, in the Bringhurst master bedroom, Alice was bent over Mrs. Bringhurst's dressing table (near the windows), looking at pictures. Rick took a picture of Alice....In the picture of Alice bent over the dressing table, in the window next to her was a dog's face looking in from outside the veranda. There were no dogs in Rockwood.

Alice related another incident that occurred on December 13, 2014, Rockwood's annual Holiday Open House. Several individuals witnessed the presence that night:

As I was standing talking to a group of guests in the Shipley reception room...I felt the presence of a dog to my left side. I started to put my hand out to pet this dog....Realizing what I was about to do and knowing there are no dogs allowed in the museum, I turned to my left and looked down to see the ghostly image of a large black dog...I then called to Linda.... Linda stepped over to the doorway and before she could say anything to me her eyes started to water....Linda then said to me, "I smell a wet dog, and I am allergic to dogs!" I then told her about my experience....Roughly ten minutes after I had left the reception room and returned to the kitchen, Ellen (docent) was stationed in the dining room....Both Ellen and Linda heard barking coming from inside the museum somewhere....No dogs were in the mansion. A few days later while I was giving a tour on the upstairs staircase where the large pictures of the Bringhurst family hang, I realized that the Irish wolfhound standing with Mary in the picture was the dog I had started to pet.

The apparition of Mary Bringhurst is believed to have also been captured in photographs, both in her second-floor bedroom and in the old butler's room on the first floor where she spent the final years of her life. In both rooms, people have reported being touched by a cold hand, and at least one visitor has fainted. But perhaps the most frightening specter to walk in Rockwood is what some have called the "Shadow Man," and his realm is the mansion's dark brick basement.

This spirit, whoever it may be, appears in the basement hallway near the old coal chutes. On paranormal tours and investigations, participants often begin to feel deeply uncomfortable in the basement, as if there is someone sinister watching them. The entity known as the Shadow Man has been photographed. Of this unnerving image, former Rockwood director Philip said on *My Ghost Story*: "The photograph down in the basement shows a man with two dark eyes. It is a very strange, unknown, dark spirit. It may be something evil, and I don't want it to be there."

On October 31, 2020, I attended a paranormal investigation on the grounds of Rockwood hosted by Rick. It was unusually cold that Halloween night. Near the end of the event, I was sitting on a stone bench beside a spirit box, which can be used to detect electronic voice phenomena. I asked a question: "Do you know why I'm here?" There were a few moments of static, and then I heard an unmistakably human-like voice say, "YES." I then asked, "May I have your permission to write about Rockwood?" This time there was no answer, only static, and I shivered. The event ended close to midnight, and as my partner and I walked to our car along the dimly lit paths, I could feel echoes of the rich history of Rockwood and its past residents all around me in the darkness.

On a Halloween 2019 episode of the local television show *The 302* about the haunting of Rockwood, host Jaccii Farris asked: "Now, you guys see ghosts all the time, here at Rockwood?" And Rick answered:

Yes, we do. It's not unusual when we're giving tours for people to see something out of the corner of their eye, where there's been a figure that's actually walked across the hallways when we've been giving tours. People's hair has been touched and moved. It happens anytime, all the time. It doesn't have to be night. It doesn't have to be day. It just happens.

Rockwood Museum and Park is an enchanted, deeply fascinating place and a priceless historic landmark of Delaware history. The fact that it is so haunted by revenants from its past does not surprise me, but I think Alice describes the immortal allure of Rockwood best:

Isn't it odd that everyone who lived in this house from 1851 to 1972 positively loved Rockwood? They never complained about any of its shortcomings in any of their writings. The last owner loved it so much she wanted to share it with visitors from all over. We can see this spirit again in the new staff and volunteers.... That's the best "spirit" of Rockwood that will never leave.

3

THE SCREAMING LADY
OF LUMS POND

L ums Pond State Park, occupying 1,790 acres of largely unspoiled
nature near the town of Bear in New Castle County, is an idyllic
place well worth visiting. Lums Pond is artificial, but it is the largest
freshwater pond in the state of Delaware. It was created in 1735 because
a dam was built at nearby St. Georges Creek to help power a newly built
gristmill. Around this time, a man named Samuel Clement built a simple
two-story brick house near the mill. The house still exists today, and it
was added to the National Register of Historic Places in 1973. Although
the mill is long gone, for many years, people have reported hearing the
unexplained churning sound of an old water wheel at the location where
the mill once stood.

Around 1809, the lands and the house were purchased by John Lum,
and the pond was eventually named after him and his family. By 1839,
Lums Pond was highly beloved in the community for providing much-
needed water to the Chesapeake and Delaware Canal. The heavily
wooded land surrounding the pond was also frequently used by enslaved
Black men and women as a route traveling north to freedom on the
Underground Railroad prior to the Civil War. It is likely that not all of
them made it out of Delaware alive, for the unmistakable sound of many
people running quickly through the dense woods is sometimes still heard
in the dead of night at Lums Pond, and shadowy human figures have
been glimpsed in the moonlight before vanishing. The area was also a
prime hunting ground for the Native Americans, so it is possible some of

View of a picnic area on the edge of Lums Pond. *Photograph by Moon Rhythm, Creative Commons License.*

the restless spirits seen in the forest belong to the tribes whose land was stolen from them.

Sometime in the mid-1950s, Lums Pond and the land surrounding it were donated to the state of Delaware. It was decided that the area would become the first state park in Delaware specifically designed to be a recreational facility for visitors. Around 1960, the pond was enlarged to its present size of two hundred acres, and Lums Pond State Park officially opened to the public in 1963.

For almost sixty years, Lums Pond State Park has been an ideal place to get away from it all and bask in the beauty of nature. The woods surrounding the pond offer seventy-four campsites for visitors to enjoy as well as picnic tables, grills and wooden pavilions for large gatherings. There are numerous sports fields throughout the park, an area for horseback riding, as well as a thrilling treetop adventure course with ziplines across the pond operated by Go Ape, which opened in 2013 to resounding success. Hunting is allowed in the park with the proper permits, as is fishing. The Swamp Forest Trail winds along 6.4 miles of the park's diverse habitats and is popular with experienced hikers, while the Little Jersey Trail is 8.0 miles long and suitable for all skill levels. You are no longer allowed to swim in Lums Pond, but you can rent paddleboats, rowboats and kayaks by the hour and enjoy being out on the water, surrounded by trees.

On a cloudy, gray, rainy day in August 2020, I did exactly that. My partner and I rented a paddleboat and made our way to the center of Lums

Pond, which looks and feels immense. It was quiet and deeply peaceful. However, if you're a horror fan like me, while sitting in the tiny boat in the middle of the water I couldn't help but think of the classic slasher movies *Friday the 13th* and *Sleepaway Camp* and what would happen if something in the water suddenly reached up from the depths to pull you under. My eyes kept being drawn to the forest that circled Lums Pond, and I wondered what secrets from the past were held in the trees' gloomy interior.

Walking along the well-kept trails through the grounds of Lums Pond State Park as the sun began to set in the west, I could not help but think about how eerie a place this would be in the dark. Once the daily visitors and park staff have gone home and no living human being is left on this immense land except for the brave souls camping in the woods for the night, how quiet it must be. No sounds except for the gentle lapping of the pond's water on the shore and the resident insects and animals of the forest. In your tent, late at night, you finally lie down to sleep with these soothing natural sounds humming all around you. You close your eyes. You breathe in deeply, and then exhale. You have never felt as relaxed and at peace as you do right now.

And then the screaming starts.

These terrifying screams of a woman fighting for her life have been heard at Lums Pond for nearly 150 years. They are still heard today. The tale behind the screams takes us back to the 1870s, long before Lums Pond became a state park. Unfortunately, the name of the woman whose story this is has not been recorded by history. But her tale has been handed down throughout the decades, resulting in a haunting that still echoes loudly in the twenty-first century.

She was a young woman of Wilmington, so the story goes, and she was running away from an abusive home. She brought nothing with her of her former life, which would be categorized as privileged to the outside eye. None of that had ever mattered to her. Not really. She took the things that she thought she needed to survive, and that was all. She heard the town clock strike the hour of midnight when she ran away from her home in Wilmington. She ran, and she ran, and she ran again. She never thought she had it in her to do this, but she did it. Finally, she found herself in the woods right by Lums Pond. This would be a perfect place to rest until daybreak. The ancient trees would protect her from harm.

But they did not protect her. For she was not alone at Lums Pond that night.

With a slow and certain dread, she realized that someone was following her as she walked through the woods in the dark. First it was the snapping of a few twigs and then the unmistakable sounds of footsteps crunching

View from the middle of Lums Pond in 2020.

the dead leaves not far behind her. She had never felt so afraid. She stopped walking, and the footsteps behind her stopped, too. She started to walk again, a little quicker this time, and the footsteps matched her pace. She stopped again, and the footsteps behind her stopped again. Then she slowly, very slowly, turned around to see what was behind her. Whoever or whatever she saw standing behind her, it made her start running away.

She screamed louder than she had ever screamed in her life, primal and piercing. Her screams echoed through the twisted trees above and around her as she ran. The insects and animals of the forest fell silent, the only witnesses. She screamed for help. And no one heard her, not then, not when it really mattered. The last thing she ever felt was the cold steel of his knife running swiftly across her throat. And then there was silence.

Her body was discovered the following morning. She was found floating in Lums Pond, naked, mutilated and bloodless. Her killer was never found. Some locals blamed the murder on a mentally ill homeless man who was known to live at Lums Pond, but nothing was ever proven. The case was closed, unsolved, and even her name is now shamefully forgotten by time.

However, this woman's spirit continues to make herself heard at Lums Pond State Park. Everyone who has heard her screams of terror in the night, her piteous begging for help and mercy, can never forget them. Many campers have left suddenly in the middle of the night due to her horrifying screams reverberating near their tents. Sometimes the police have been called and the woods searched thoroughly, but nothing and no one is ever found.

Lums Pond State Park is an idyllic place, and I recommend it highly. But like many places in the state of Delaware, the history of the land has left tangible echoes in the present. Pitch your tent right by Lums Pond some night. Have a campfire and roast some marshmallows. Listen to the insects and the animals of the forest humming around you. It is so peaceful here, isn't it?

And then the screaming starts.

4

A HEADLESS HORSEMAN IN NEWARK

The dominant spirit, however, that haunts this enchanted region...is the apparition of a figure on horseback, without a head. It is said by some to be the ghost of a Hessian trooper, whose head had been carried away by a cannonball, in some nameless battle during the Revolutionary War, and who is ever and anon seen by the country folk hurrying along in the gloom of night, as if on the wings of the wind. His haunts are not confined to the valley, but extend at times to the adjacent roads, and especially to the vicinity of a church at no great distance. Indeed, certain of the most authentic historians of those parts, who have been careful in collecting and collating the floating facts concerning this specter, allege that the body of the trooper having been buried in the churchyard, the ghost rides forth to the scene of battle in nightly quest of his head, and that the rushing speed with which he sometimes passes along the Hollow, like a midnight blast, is owing to his being...in a hurry to get back to the churchyard before daybreak. Such is the general purport of this legendary superstition, which has furnished materials for many a wild story in that region of shadows; and the specter is known at all the country firesides, by the name of the Headless Horseman.

Thus, begins one of the greatest of all Halloween campfire tales, "The Legend of Sleepy Hollow," written by Washington Irving in 1820. What most Delawareans do not know is that there is a strikingly similar legend right here in the town of Newark. This tale has been told for centuries, almost since the end of the American Revolution, long before Washington Irving wrote his own famous ghost story. That's right: the state of Delaware has its own real Headless Horseman.

On a lonely stretch of road in New Castle County there stands the Welsh Tract Old School Baptist Church. In 1701, a group of Welsh Baptists settled in Philadelphia near Pennypack Creek and joined the local congregation there. However, the Welsh Baptists did not get along with the Philadelphia Baptists. In the church meeting records, the following quote was translated:

We could not be in fellowship (at the Lord's table) with our brethren in Pennypack and Philadelphia, because they did not hold to the laying on of hands, and some other particulars relating to a church; true, some of them believed in the ordinance, but neither preached it nor practiced it; and when we moved to Welsh Tract, and left twenty-two of our members at Pennypack, and took some of their members down with us, the difficulty increased.

In 1703, the Welsh Baptists purchased thirty thousand acres in what would eventually be known as Newark, Delaware, from William Penn. Along what is now called Welsh Tract Road, they built a small church and began to bury their dead there. The church that currently stands on top of a small hill, surrounded by decaying tombstones, was built in 1746 using timbers from the earlier church. Added to the National Register of Historic Places in 1973, its nomination form says:

Welsh Tract Old School Baptist Church is a simple rectangular brick building with a wood shingled jerkinhead roof....Tombstones dating to the first half of the eighteenth century, some of native rock, survive in the surrounding graveyard. The interior furnishings are Victorian....A badly mended portion of one wall is said to be the result of a cannonball shot when the British encountered American militia at Cooch's Bridge in September of 1777.

This strange patchwork of brick on the church is a physical scar of the night when a soldier lost his head, and a ghostly legend was born.

The only Revolutionary War battle fought on Delaware's soil was the Battle of Cooch's Bridge on September 3, 1777. The battle began around nine o'clock in the morning and lasted for over seven hours, ending with the sunset. It was primarily fought between American militia and German soldiers who were fighting for the British army. It has long been said that the Battle of Cooch's Bridge was the first time the newly adopted American flag was flown during the American Revolution, although historians have so far been unable to definitively prove it.

The church, with repaired brickwork from a cannonball, and the graveyard.

Lieutenant General William Howe and Major General George Washington were the leaders of the two armies. In the days leading up to the Battle of Cooch's Bridge, both forces were camped close enough that they were able to observe one another. A Hessian soldier wrote: "These gentlemen observed us with their glasses as carefully as we observed them."

As the day dawned on September 3, 1777, Captain Johann Ewald and a small company of German soldiers advanced toward Cooch's Bridge. American soldiers were waiting in the woods to ambush them, and most of the German soldiers were killed. Captain Ewald escaped unwounded and reported to Howe, the Americans reported to Brigadier General William Maxwell and soon the battle began. Major John André wrote: "Here the rebels began to attack us about 9 o'clock with a continued irregular fire for nearly two miles."

The Americans were greatly outnumbered. When they ran out of bullets, they attacked the Hessians with bayonets, swords and their bare hands. Finally, they were forced to retreat over Cooch's Bridge, which was described as decrepit even then, and take shelter in Wilmington. The number of soldiers killed and wounded in the Battle of Cooch's Bridge is not certain. According to the British, forty-one Americans were killed and many more were wounded. Americans said twenty were killed and another twenty wounded. George Washington summarized the battle in one of his many letters to Congress: "This morning the Enemy came out with considerable force and three pieces of artillery, against our light advanced corps, and after some pretty smart skirmishing obliged them to retreat, being far inferior in number and without cannon."

Legend has it, and there is tangible proof on the western wall of Welsh Tract Old School Baptist Church, that one of those cannonballs fired by the Hessians beheaded a young soldier and created a ghost story. Master storyteller and historian Ed Okonowicz writes in *Pulling Back the Curtain*,

A drawing of Captain Johann von Ewald in 1835. *C.A. Jensen, public domain.*

the first book in his series about Delaware ghost stories, that the name of Newark's Headless Horseman was Charlie Miller. He was a young man, the son of a grain merchant, who wanted nothing more than to defend his country. As soon as he was old enough, he enlisted in the American army and wore his uniform proudly. He longed for the chance to prove his love for country on the field of battle. On September 3, 1777, Charlie Miller got his wish.

He was not prepared for how loud the Hessian cannons were or for the sights of blood and gaping wounds on his fallen comrades. He was not prepared to hear the screams of agony from his friends as a cannonball took off an arm, a leg, a head. Seeing all this, Charlie Miller thought for a moment of his mother, who had begged him not to go fight in the war. And then he had a more unsettling thought: "How many of these men here will never see their mothers again?"

As Charlie Miller was thinking these thoughts, a cannonball was making its way toward his head. He did not see it coming. It hit the back of his skull, and then he knew no more. In an instant, Charlie Miller's headless corpse fell from his white horse onto the ground and he watered the land with his blood. His head was never found, and his white horse was never recovered. But the cannonball that decapitated Charlie Miller finally connected with the western wall of Welsh Tract Old School Baptist Church. Some say his headless body was buried in an unmarked grave in the church's cemetery. Cooch's Bridge collapsed before the end of the American Revolution and was never rebuilt.

Ever since that night of September 3, 1777, the specter of Charlie Miller has haunted the vicinity of Welsh Tract Road, often appearing on moonlit autumn nights. People have heard the sound of heavy hoofbeats along the dark road when there are no horses to be seen. In the modern era, it has been noted that the stretch of Welsh Tract Road that runs by the church and graveyard has a much higher number of automobile accidents than any other road in the vicinity. Over the years, more than one person has gone on the record saying they crashed their car because they saw something strange suddenly emerge from the woods. All of them describe a white horse ridden by the shadowy figure of man without a head. Sometimes, the apparition merely appears on the side of the road, but some people have reported seeing a headless horseman following their cars down the road until they pass by the old church and graveyard.

Today, Welsh Tract Old School Baptist Church looks much like it did back when the Battle of Cooch's Bridge took place in 1777. The church is still active and holds services on the second Sunday of every month. Visiting the site on an overcast, gloomy day, as I did, it does have the look and feel of a haunted place. The graveyard, with its rotting tombstones and overgrown grass, looks like the perfect spooky cemetery of your imagination. It was easy for me to imagine how frightening a place this could be at night.

The lonely, overgrown graveyard.

On a moonlit evening in the autumn, near or on the anniversary of the Battle of Cooch's Bridge, you could pass by the old church on the dark hill of Welsh Tract Road and you might see, standing among the gravestones, on his white spectral steed, the ghost of Charlie Miller, the Headless Horseman of Newark, Delaware, still searching for another head to replace the one ripped away so many years ago. If you should see him there, drive away as quickly as you can. For the dead travel fast.

5

THE LEGEND OF
FIDDLER'S BRIDGE

A n intriguing article appeared in the *Wilmington Sunday Star* newspaper on October 4, 1953, just in time for Halloween. It was a contemporary update on one of Delaware's most enduring and most disturbing ghost stories: the legend of Fiddler's Bridge. The text was written by "F.M." and is accompanied by an illustration depicting the famous ghost that would never be allowed to go to print today. Nonetheless, the article is worth quoting for its evocative writing as well as being a snapshot of the legend as it stood in the mid-twentieth century. The article's title is "Ghost Fiddler Loses Spirit" with the subtitle "Legend Doesn't Say So, but the Fiddler of Fiddler's Bridge May Well Have Given Up the Ghost in Disgust." Here's how the article begins:

The ghost with the lowest spirits in Delaware right now probably is the one who hangs out—or used to hang out—under Fiddler's Bridge down St. Georges way. This ghost once had a lucrative little trade. It operated a sort of spectral jukebox. Legend said that if exactly at midnight a passerby dropped a coin over the bridge rail into the stream below, the ghost of an old Negro fiddle player who was drowned there long ago would play a medley of sweet music. But that was before the automobile age, when the bridge was narrow and lonely, and the road passed through a dismal swamp. The road has long since been widened into the DuPont dual highway (Route 13) and the bridge, which spans Scott's Run a short distance below the C and D canal at St. Georges, has been transformed into a thing of macadam and reinforced concrete. Legend doesn't say what the fiddling ghost thought of these renovations, but the chances are he wasn't pleased. After all, it couldn't have been much fun, sitting under that dank concrete and bracing the ectoplasm against the rumble of ten-ton tractor-trailers overhead. Even if a motorist did stop and drop in a coin, the ghost probably couldn't have made his eerie music heard above the roar of traffic. No one could blame him if he finally gave up the ghost business in disgust, thus becoming Delaware folklore's first traffic casualty. Nowadays, motorists whizz over the bridge without realizing it is there, for it is scarcely more than a large culvert in the highway. But, below, Scott's Run meanders on as of old, choked with weeds and watercress, still an ideal place for ghostly concerts.

The legend of the phantom fiddler also appeared in print fifteen years earlier, in the 1938 book *Delaware: A Guide to the First State*. It says of the Fiddler's Bridge haunting:

Fiddler's Bridge…was once a narrow crossing where the swamp trees met densely overhead—a dark and gloomy place. There is a tradition that a demented Negro fiddler used to sit on the bridge rail and play doleful tunes. One night he fell in and was drowned. For generations it has been said that if precisely at midnight a silver coin is dropped into the water, the fiddler will play.

There are stories of ghostly encounters at Fiddler's Bridge going back to the 1890s. In one tale dating from that period, a wealthy man from Delaware City held a grand party. After his guests had eaten and drunk and the hours crept toward midnight, he told his guests the chilling legend of the fiddler's ghost. He insisted that those who were brave follow him to the bridge to see if they could make the fiddler play his music. Nearly all the guests took up the challenge, and they followed their host down the dark wooded path to the haunted bridge. It seemed unnaturally quiet as the midnight hour came, and the silence was broken only by the sound of a silver coin being thrown into the dark, murky water. A few moments passed, and the guests began to laugh in relief. But then the silence was broken again by the sound of soft, mournful music drifting on the wind, coming from somewhere close at hand.

Naturally, the guests all fled in terror from the ghostly music, running back through the woods as fast as their feet could carry them. The host laughed loudly all the way home, for he had played a devious trick. He had told one of his Black servants to wait under the bridge and play a

The location of Fiddler's Bridge at Scott's Run, as seen in the early twentieth century before the highway was built. *Delaware Public Archives.*

fiddle when he heard the coin fall into the water. The host had succeeded in frightening his friends out of their minds, and he was extremely pleased with himself. It had all gone perfectly. When the host returned to the house, he went to the servant's quarters to congratulate the fake phantom musician on a job well done.

Then it was the host's turn to be afraid. His servant was sick and had never left the house that night. The ghostly music he and his friends had heard that midnight at Fiddler's Bridge was real.

———— • ————

SO, WE KNOW FROM the stories handed down that there was a ghost haunting Fiddler's Bridge by the end of the nineteenth century. But how did the Black fiddle player become a ghost in the first place? This legendary haunting also illuminates some of the most horrific aspects of Delaware's real history.

Delaware was a slave state that stayed with the Union during the Civil War, and its relationship with racism has always been complex and contradictory. The first known Black person in what would become the state of Delaware was a man given the name Anthony. He was captured in the West Indies by the captain of a Swedish ship called the *Vogel Grip* and forcibly taken to New Sweden, an area that would eventually become the city of Wilmington. He arrived on this soil as an enslaved man, but according to historical records, by the 1650s "Black Anthony" was a free Black man going by the name Antoni Swart and working for state governor Johan Printz.

The Delaware state constitution of 1776 ordered, "No person hereafter imported to this state from Africa ought to be held in slavery under any pretense whatever." However, this did not free the Black people already enslaved in Delaware or their children born into slavery, and there were many free Black citizens who were kidnapped and sold illegally by their white neighbors. Nineteenth-century men of Delaware fought in both Union armies and Confederate, although Delaware did not have any official Confederate regiments. Because of its proximity to the free state of Pennsylvania, Delaware was a pivotal stop on the Underground Railroad. But there was also a reverse Underground Railroad that sold Black people south. The most notorious perpetrator of this atrocity was Patty Cannon, Delaware's first known serial killer, whose grisly tale will be told in a subsequent chapter.

In 1790, there were approximately 9,000 enslaved Black people living in Delaware. By 1861, when the Civil War began, there were 1,798 and the majority of Delaware's Black population were free. When the war ended, all enslaved people in the state were effectively freed from bondage. However, Delaware also initially rejected the Thirteenth, Fourteenth and Fifteenth Amendments to the Constitution and did not ratify them until 1901.

Delaware was also the last state in America to abolish whipping as a form of capital punishment, finally doing so in 1972. The last public whipping in Delaware had occurred twenty years earlier, in 1952. Between 1900 and 1945 alone, 1,604 prisoners were whipped in Delaware, and it is a matter of historical record that the majority of them were Black. All whippings were required by law to be public, usually on Saturday afternoons, and were sometimes attended by thousands of people. Some called the whipping posts a "Red Hannah" due to the human blood that would stain the wood as the prisoner had their arms chained around it, "hugging Red Hannah" as they received up to forty unmerciful lashes. Sometimes, the ears of the prisoner would be also be nailed to the post before the whipping, causing even greater

A combined "Red Hannah" whipping post and pillory at the New Castle County Jail in 1907. *Library of Congress.*

physical agony and emotional humiliation as the crowds looked on. The final Delaware whipping post was removed from public display in front of the Old Sussex County Courthouse in Georgetown on July 1, 2020. It had been installed at that location as a historic monument in 1993.

From this historical truth, the ghostly legend of Fiddler's Bridge was born.

————◆————

THIS TALE BEGINS IN the early part of the nineteenth century before the Civil War, as far as any of the old-timers can tell. Back in those days, there was a farm at Scott's Run owned by a White man named Osborn. Mr. Osborn had slaves, two of whom were man and wife, who had been abducted from Africa to Delaware. They had a child, a smiling baby boy they named Jacob.

From a young age, little Jacob was in love with music. He was always making music with whatever he could find, and when he got older, he made himself a fiddle out of tree branches, string and a box, and he played that homemade fiddle like it was the most exquisite violin. His mother and father loved to hear him play music at night, and soon people came from all over the county to hear Jacob's masterful fiddling. One morning, Jacob awoke to discover an expensive real fiddle had been left for him outside the house. He never found out who gave him this great gift but repaid it by making heavenly music.

The one person who hated the sound of Jacob's music was Mr. Osborn. One night, as Jacob was playing his fiddle, an enraged Osborn whipped Jacob until he was unconscious and bleeding from the ears to silence his voice forever. For days after the savage beating, Jacob was delirious, and his mother and father cared for him as best they could. Jacob eventually regained consciousness, but he never spoke a single word again. Instead, he picked up his beloved fiddle and began to play.

All Jacob ever did now was play his fiddle, but his music had changed. Before the whipping by Mr. Osborn, the tunes Jacob played had been joyous, but now sadness seemed to vibrate from every note he sounded with his bow. But even in its deep melancholy, Jacob's music was still beautiful. He went away to live in the woods nearby, under the bridge at Scott's Run. Mr. Osborn, seeing the grief his violence had caused, did nothing to prevent Jacob from leaving.

Jacob never left the bridge, and he never stopped playing his fiddle. His mother and father brought him food and would listen to their son's haunting music. Everyone who lived around the bridge could hear the music, and on many moonlit nights people would pause and listen to Jacob play. Sometimes people passing by would throw a silver coin at Jacob's feet in thanks. He would smile, give a friendly nod and then go back to his fiddle.

One dark night, at midnight, the fiddle playing suddenly stopped. The following morning, Jacob's parents went to the bridge to deliver his breakfast. They found their son's drowned body lying facedown in the water underneath the bridge, his precious fiddle still clutched tightly in his hands.

His parents buried him with it.

Had Jacob fallen into the river accidentally, or was there a more sinister cause for his death?

No one ever knew.

Not long after Jacob's funeral, several men happened to be walking by the bridge around midnight on their way home. They paused at the bridge, which was now lonely and silent. In remembrance of Jacob, one of the men tossed a silver coin into the water below. And after a few moments, they heard something impossible. Their skin burst out in goosebumps because what they were hearing was music—the beautiful music of Jacob and his fiddle drifting out from the darkness of the night.

Ever since then, so the legend goes, anyone who is brave enough to throw a silver coin in the river at Scott's Run on the stroke of midnight will hear the same unearthly melodies that have echoed around Fiddler's Bridge for generations. Even with the constant flow of twenty-first-century traffic on the highway above, I believe there still exists the specter of a Black man perhaps named Jacob, still playing his supernatural symphony, his voice still refusing to be silenced.

6

DARK ENTITIES ON DOVER GREEN

On September 11, 1778, a French soldier named Louis Philippe visited the city of Dover, Delaware, for the first time. A relative of the Marquis de Lafayette, Louis Philippe wrote about his initial impressions of Dover in his *Memoirs and Recollections*:

> *I set out early in the morning for Philadelphia, and I could therefore only see Dover in passing....Its appearance struck me; it was surrounded by thick woods because there, as in other parts of the thirteen states, the population was still scattered over an immense territory, a small portion of which was cultivated. All the houses in Dover offered a simple but elegant appearance. They were built of wood and painted with different colors. The variety in their aspect, the neatness which distinguished them, the bright and polished knockers of the doors, seemed all to announce the order and activity, the intelligence and prosperity of the inhabitants.*

Only one year earlier, on May 12, 1777, Dover had become the new capital of Delaware. Located at the exact heart of the state, the city of Dover was created by William Penn in 1683 and named after the town of Dover in Kent, England. It was the home of Caesar Rodney, who famously made a last-minute journey back to Philadelphia to cast Delaware's tie-breaking vote in favor of American Independence. The old historic district of Dover has been lovingly preserved over time and is now known as First State Heritage Park. Walking around the park, it is incredibly easy to forget you are in the

A tree standing on the Dover Green.

twenty-first century. The Old State House, the Kent County Courthouse, the Bradford-Loockerman House and the Parke Ridgely House all stand in the same spots they have occupied since the eighteenth century. The Golden Fleece Tavern is also a notable historic location—it was there that a group of thirty delegates voted to ratify the U.S. Constitution on December 7, 1787, thus making Delaware the First State.

Life in colonial Dover was centered on the Green, a peaceful square of landscaped grass and tall trees originally established as Court House Square in 1722. Market days were held on the Green, and it is also the location where the troops held their final muster before going off to fight bravely during the American Revolution. With so much history compressed within a small location, it is no surprise that the Green is haunted by several restless souls from days gone by that refuse to rest in peace.

The most famous ghost story connected with the Dover Green is that of Samuel Chew. Born on Halloween Eve—October 30, 1693—Samuel Chew grew up on his family's estate Maidstone in what is now called Calvert County, Maryland. Maidstone, which still exists today, is also haunted by the apparition of a Gray Lady. Samuel Chew trained as a physician, and in 1715 he married a woman named Mary Galloway. Tragically, after nineteen happy years of marriage, Mary Galloway Chew died in 1734. After his wife's sudden death, Samuel Chew needed a change of scenery. He moved to Kent County, Delaware, in 1738 and built a mansion known as Whitehall, which was a plantation supported by the back-breaking labor of enslaved Black people. Just three years later, in 1741, Pennsylvania governor John Penn made Samuel Chew the chief justice of Delaware. A devout Quaker since birth, Chew was excommunicated by the Friends for supporting the French and Indian War.

In between cases, Samuel Chew was often seen sitting or walking on the Green in Dover, dressed in his customary black robes and white wig. It was

Maidstone Plantation, the birthplace of Samuel Chew. *Photograph by Karl Whittington, Creative Commons License.*

during this time that many people in town began to mock Chew for no other reason than his last name. When passing by him, folks would often produce loud and artificial sneezes—ACHOO!—and make obnoxious chewing sounds with their mouths. This happened every time Samuel Chew appeared on the Dover Green, but he never once gave an offender the satisfaction of becoming upset in public.

However, everyone who has ever been bullied about something so stupid as the name they were given at birth has probably thought at least once: "I will come back to haunt you after I die, and you will know no peace." According to stories passed down, Samuel Chew did exactly that.

Samuel Chew died on June 16, 1743, at the age of fifty. It is said that people sneezed and masticated during his funeral. Not long after that, his ghost began to be seen in the dark of the night on the Dover Green, seen only by the men who had so mercilessly made fun of him when he was alive. This haunting went on for two years after his death. The 1938 book *Delaware: A Guide to the First State*, tells the tale of this most unusual haunting in its chapter on the Green:

Here took place, in 1745, the laying of the restless ghost of Chief Justice Samuel Chew by public ceremony....Late one night a rustic on his way home over The Green was astonished to see a shadowy figure under a poplar tree. Upon drawing nearer, he recognized it as the late Chief Justice, standing in his favorite attitude, head bowed in deep meditation. By coincidence, the local miller crossed The Green at the same spot just a few nights later, and there stood the dim figure of the Chief Justice under the same poplar tree. But this time the jurist beckoned to the miller. So generally believed were these tales that Dover residents took to staying home of nights, to the dismay of tavern-keepers and shopkeepers.

After two years of being haunted by the ghost of Samuel Chew, Dover residents decided they had had enough. A group of brave souls met one night at the Eagle Tavern, and after several rounds of liquid courage, they came up with a plan to end the haunting and apologize for their cruel treatment of Samuel Chew. The next morning, no doubt nursing hangovers, these citizens of Dover dug a grave six feet deep at the roots of the poplar tree where Samuel Chew's ghost had appeared on the Green. Six of the men who had bullied Chew in life carried an empty wooden coffin to the site, processing as the church bells rang loudly in the morning air. As the terrorized citizens of Dover looked on, the empty coffin was buried in the earth. Finally, Samuel Chew was laid to rest for the second time, and his ghost was not seen again.

And yet, many people who have walked the Green in Dover in recent years have reported seeing Samuel Chew's unearthly apparition dressed in his judge's robes, suggesting that the exorcism was not permanent. And his is not the only phantom reported at that location after dark. There is another one, whose story is the stuff of nightmares.

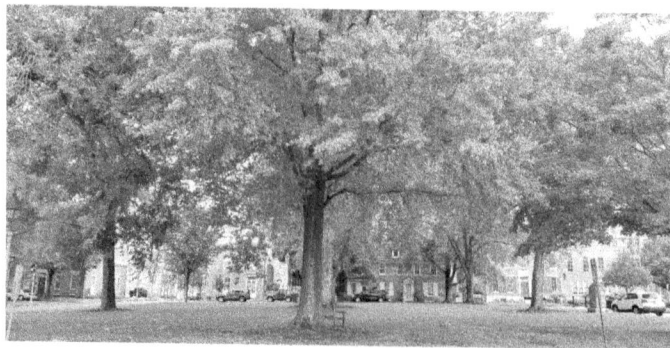

The final resting place of a ghost?

On December 4, 1872, a man named Isaac West murdered another man named Couch Turn. They lived together on Loockerman Street in Dover, near the Green. The nature of their relationship is not recorded by history. It is known that Isaac West bludgeoned Couch Turn to death with a hammer. After that, he skinned Turn's corpse. Then he set fire to the building they lived in, trying to make it look like an accident. Isaac West was tried for murder, but due to all the physical evidence successfully destroyed in the fire, he was acquitted.

Some say that if you happen to be on the Green on the cold winter night of December 4, you may encounter the specter of the bloody, de-fleshed phantom of Couch Turner, who is still waiting for justice, heard screaming in Dover on the anniversary of his brutal murder. Not only does Delaware boast a real Headless Horseman, but Delaware also has its own Skinless Ghost.

7
FOUR WRAITHS AT WOODBURN

J ust a short walk away from the ghostly environs of the Dover Green, at the intersection of King's Highway and Pennsylvania Avenue, you will find the mansion known as Woodburn. It has been the residence of the governor of Delaware since it was purchased by the state in 1965, but the eerie history of Woodburn goes back far earlier than that. You see, Woodburn, like the Rockwood Mansion, is known as one of Delaware's most haunted houses.

In 1784, an affluent landowner named Charles Hillyard III purchased the land on which Woodburn now stands for $110 at a sheriff's sale. Hillyard was a fourth-generation Delawarean, and his family had long been active in the politics and social life of Dover and the surrounding area of Kent County. Around 1790, Charles Hillyard III built a grand mansion on King's Highway, and he christened it Woodburn.

Delaware author George Alfred Townsend wrote briefly of Woodburn and its first occupant Charles Hillyard III in his bestselling book *The Entailed Hat*. While presented as a novel about the notorious Patty Cannon (about whom you shall hear more very soon), *The Entailed Hat* is also based mostly on truth and facts gleaned from interviews with people who knew the subjects involved. Townsend writes that Charles Hillyard III was

a tyrannical, eccentric man who, it was said, amused himself by making his own children stand on their toes, switching their feet with a whip when they dropped upon their soles with pain and fatigue. His own son finally

Woodburn as it
appeared in 1959.
*Photograph by Cortland
Van Dyke Hubbard.*

*shot at him through the great northern door with a rifle or pistol, leaving its
mark to this day to be seen by a small panel set in the original pine.*

While based on historical fact, George Alfred Townsend was known to
exaggerate a bit in *The Entailed Hat*, so we may take that tale with a grain
of salt. However, there *is* a repaired section of that door at Woodburn that
is still visible, and there is yet another version of how the bullet got there.
In his 1824 book *Recollections of Dover*, Judge George Purnell Fisher claimed
that the gun was fired by Charles Hillyard III himself, attempting to
murder one of his own sons in a wild drunken rage. Whatever happened,
Charles Hillyard III died in 1814 and Woodburn passed into the hands of
his daughter Mary, who moved into the house with her husband, Martin
W. Bates, a lawyer who would eventually become a U.S. senator.

The haunting of Woodburn began one year after Mary and Martin
Bates moved into the house. In 1815, the Bateses were entertaining a guest
in the home, a well-known traveling Methodist preacher by the name of
Lorenzo Dow. While on his way downstairs for breakfast one morning,
Dow met an old man on the staircase he had never seen before. The old
man was dressed strangely, in clothing that seemed old-fashioned. Dow
nodded at the old man, and the old man nodded back at Dow. Then the
preacher walked down the stairs and into the luxurious dining room where
Mary and Martin Bates awaited him.

They asked Lorenzo Dow to say grace before they dived into their
breakfast, but Dow said, "Surely we should wait for the other guest?" Mary
and Martin Bates exchanged a confused, worried look between them. Martin

71

Bates asked, "What other guest?" Dow explained that they should wait for the old man he just met on the staircase and then described the old man's strange, old-fashioned appearance. Mary Hillyard Bates's face grew pale as she listened to Lorenzo Dow speak. Finally, she looked Dow in the eye and said very slowly and quietly, "There is no other guest in this house, Mr. Dow. From what you describe, that was my father, Charles Hillyard III, that you saw. He has been dead in his grave for a year now."

Mary and Martin Bates made Lorenzo Dow swear that he would never tell another living soul about what he had seen in the house, and they never invited him to stay at Woodburn again. Fortunately for us, Lorenzo Dow did talk about his ghostly experience, and it has become part of the house's eerie history.

Perhaps because of the presence of her father's ghost, Mary Hillyard Bates sold Woodburn in 1825 to a man named Daniel Cowgill. He was a Quaker and an abolitionist who had freed the enslaved Africans in his family's possession from bondage. Cowgill encouraged both free and enslaved Black people to use Woodburn as a safe meeting place, and he went even further. Daniel Cowgill also built a secret tunnel (now sealed) leading from the house's basement to the nearby river, making Woodburn an important stop on the Underground Railroad. It is from this time that another ghostly legend of the house was born.

In George Alfred Townsend's *The Entailed Hat*, he describes several members of Patty Cannon's gang converging at the "Cowgill House" around midnight, intending to kidnap the Black men and women meeting there and sell them South. It is a dark and foggy night when the gang arrives. Fortunately, Daniel Cowgill is prepared for them. A few shots from his rifle manage to scare the nefarious gang members away—all except one. One stays behind, hiding in the tall branches of a poplar tree beside the house. He waits until Woodburn is quiet and then breaks into the cellar where he knows Black bodies are being sheltered.

However, in a stroke of macabre justice, the man slips and begins to fall from the tree. But he never makes it to the ground. Instead, the man's neck becomes wedged between two branches as he falls. The force is not great enough to break his neck immediately, which would have given him a quick and merciful death. Oh no—over a period of as long as an hour the racist slave hunter strangles to death between the branches in slow agony. The sounds of him choking are either unheard by those inside the house or purposefully ignored. His lifeless corpse is cut down from the poplar tree the next day, his face a frozen mask of pain and terror.

Ever since the night Townsend immortalized, the poplar tree next to Woodburn was known as "The Hanging Tree," and many a Dover denizen who walked past the old mansion on dark and foggy nights would hear the unmistakable and hideous sound of a man choking, strangling, gasping for his last breaths. This old, tall, twisted tree was cut down in 1999, apparently for "safety concerns." No one has heard the sickening strangling sounds since the tree was removed over twenty years ago.

The ghost of Charles Hillyard III, however, has continued to be seen throughout the years. In 1918, Woodburn was sold to a dentist from Philadelphia by the name of Frank Hall, who conducted many renovations of the house during the time he lived there. These renovations were apparently not approved of by the ghost of Charles Hillyard III, the man who built Woodburn. One night, a male friend of Frank Hall's was staying in the house as a guest. The room given to him was the bedroom Hillyard had died in over one hundred years ago. Frank said goodnight to his friend and was walking to his own room when he heard his friend scream in horror. Hall ran to find his friend unconscious on the floor outside of Hillyard's bedroom. When he regained consciousness, the friend told Hall that he had opened the bedroom door and saw an old man in strange clothes sitting by the fireplace. The old man looked right at him, then stood up and began to walk slowly toward him. That was what made the friend faint dead away. Strangely, when Frank Hall found him, the bedroom door had shut and was somehow locked from the inside.

After this event, Frank Hall decided to sleep in the bedroom himself. During the night he awoke from a deep sleep to the sound of someone knocking on his bedroom door. Hall got out of bed and unlocked and opened the door—to find no one there. He closed the door, locked it and returned to bed. Twice more that night he heard someone knocking, and both times there was no one behind the door. He locked it again. When Frank Hall awoke the next morning, having only gotten a few hours of restless sleep, he saw that the bedroom door he had locked so carefully was now wide open. Then there was a second unsettling discovery. His glasses, which he had kept on the bedside table, where now by the open door, and they had been smashed to pieces. After these occurrences, Frank Hall called Charles Hillyard III's bedroom "The Ghost Room." Until he finally sold Woodburn in 1953, Hall would refuse to ever allow anyone to sleep in that room, and he always made sure it was locked.

It was after Frank Hall's residence ended in 1953 that people began to whisper about the possibility of Woodburn becoming Delaware's Governor's

Woodburn as it
appears today.

Mansion. Ed Okonowicz writes in *Opening the Door*, his second book in the *Spirits Between the Bays* series, about this turning point in Woodburn's history:

When the state was considering the purchase of Woodburn, the late Bill Frank, well-known Delaware journalist, wrote several stories about the Dover home, and included a number of details about its legends and ghosts. Frank expressed positive opinions about the state's need for a governor's mansion and, in one of his "Frankly Speaking" columns, wrote: "Woodburn is a beautiful house. If it is available for $65,000 more or less, it's a bargain and should somehow be preserved as a public building—ghosts and all."

The State of Delaware did indeed purchase Woodburn for that price in 1965, making it the official residence of the governor. In addition, $70,000 was spent on repairs and renovations restoring Woodburn to its eighteenth-century splendor. The mansion opened to the public for tours the following year, 1966. That same year, Jessica Irby Terry, wife of Charles L. Terry, the first governor to live at Woodburn, said to a reporter with some pride: "So you've heard about our ghosts. It's such fun to live in a place that's distinguished enough to have legends. In England, every house worth its history has a ghost or two."

Jessica Irby Terry was the first of many of have subsequently reported a haunting in the dining room at Woodburn. The sound of unexplained footsteps walking in the dining room has been heard when the room should have been empty. From time to time, the vivid apparition of a Revolutionary War soldier in full uniform has been seen in the dining room, often drinking a glass of wine. This spirit has been nicknamed "The Tippling Ghost," because wine glasses left unfinished in the dining room at night have been found mysteriously emptied when people go to collect them the next morning. Jeanne Tribbitt, wife of 1970s governor Sherman Tribbitt, even left glasses of wine in the dining room overnight on purpose, hoping to catch a glimpse of the ghost. Apparently, the Tippling Ghost never took her bait. She is quoted on Woodburn's official website expressing her disappointment, saying, "I made sure that I didn't even tell my husband I was doing this, or he would have drank the wine just to tease me!"

Woodburn was used as a temporary hospital during the American Revolution, so it is possible that the Tippling Ghost is one of the soldiers who sadly succumbed to his battle wounds inside the house over two hundred years ago. But now, at least he seems to be enjoying his time at Woodburn in the afterlife.

The final specter to haunt Woodburn is the ghost of a young girl who has been seen wearing a red gingham dress and a bonnet—clothes from another time. No one knows her name or how she came to haunt the mansion and its grounds, but she continues to be seen. Governor Charles Terry first reported seeing her in the kitchen in the late 1960s and also hearing the sound of little footsteps running away when he would enter a room, even though no children were living at Woodburn during that time. Most frequently, the phantom of the little girl is seen outside in the lush gardens behind the house, sometimes playing and sometimes carrying a burning candle in her hands at dusk as she walks around the reflecting pool and fountain over and over and over again. Sometimes, at night, people have heard and seen the water in the fountain being splashed by tiny invisible hands.

When Governor Michael Castle was inaugurated in 1985, dozens of guests encountered the ghost of the little girl in the red gingham dress on that eventful day. Many people felt their pants or dresses tugged on

The garden of Woodburn, where a ghostly girl plays around the fountain.

from a low height, like a child trying to get their attention. During the ceremony itself, the apparition of the little girl was seen standing shyly in a corner by many witnesses while Governor Castle was sworn in.

With over two centuries of history echoing within its beautiful walls, Woodburn is indeed a mansion fit for the governor of Delaware, and I am sure its four resident wraiths would agree.

8

THE VANISHING BOARDWALK

The 1938 Federal Writers' Project book *Delaware: A Guide to the First State* describes Woodland Beach like this:

> *Woodland Beach is a small fishing, bathing, and picnicking resort (boats and fishing equipment for hire) in a grove occupying a high and dry spot on the bay shore of marshy Bombay Hook Island...which is separated from the mainland by Old Duck Creek. Summer residents live in small cottages and boarding houses. Hundreds of weekend anglers from the cities join the farm families who come for the day....By legend this lonely and windswept beach was chosen by Captain William Kidd as a cache for plunder; digging for it, however, has been in vain.*

Even back in 1938, the unincorporated community of Woodland Beach near the town of Smyrna in Kent County, Delaware, was a ghost of its former self. However, the tiny community nestled snugly along the water of the Delaware Bay still survives today, and it is one of those hidden places in the First State locals and tourists are drawn to, if they know where to look.

There is only one way to drive to Woodland Beach. You travel along Delaware's Route 6, now called Woodland Beach Road, as far as you can go. As you get closer to your final destination, you will notice the road is barely elevated over the watery marshland visible from your car's windows.

The fishing pier at Woodland Beach.

Then you see a yellow permanent sign that tells you there is water on the road ahead. I know from experience you should listen to that sign if it has been raining all day, as it had been when I visited Woodland Beach in the midst of a rainstorm in the summer of 2020.

My partner was driving the car, and I sat beside him in the front seat with my eyes closed, praying we'd get past the flooding on the road. After several long minutes of dread, we made it through the water and arrived at Woodland Beach just in time for sunset. You see, that is when the ghosts are supposed to come out.

In the nineteenth century, Delaware's Woodland Beach was what Rehoboth Beach has become in the present day. Back then, Woodland Beach was known as the "playground of Kent County." It was a resort where both the elite and the ordinary could gather, together, in the summer. In those halcyon days, the little community of Woodland Beach, Delaware, boasted a hotel called Woodland Park, a two-story pavilion featuring dancing and a live band and, crucially, its own tavern. There was also a boardwalk along the water with places to dine, games and many rides, including a rollercoaster that took its courageous riders over the Delaware Bay itself.

All that marvelous splendor ended at Woodland Beach on October 23, 1878, when a hurricane caused unprecedented destruction throughout the state of Delaware the week prior to Halloween. At least one hundred people were killed, along with countless animals drowned and millions of dollars in property damage.

The *Daily Gazette* newspaper published an article called "Storm in Kent County" on November 1, 1878, that reported the horrific tidal wave that all but destroyed the resort of Woodland Beach, which was also sometimes known as "Fraland":

Bombay Hook was swept from end to end and for the past week has presented the appearance of a vast lake....The only communication with the Island has been by boat. Persons on the west of the Island saw the big wave when it mounted the beach and noted its bank, and it was not until they heard the angry roar of splashing waters that they realized the destruction in its wake, and fled for the mainland. As it was, two children of Hugh Durham were drowned aged 3 and 9 years, and he at one time was in water up to his neck. The destruction of property has been immense....The dwelling of Lewis Campbell was moved from its foundation, the waters running through the lower rooms and waves dashing into the second story windows. The kitchen was moved 50 feet from the house....Samuel Loatman lives on the highest point of the Island ten or twelve feet above bay-level and the water came up within a few feet of his house. "Fraland" is nearly ruined; all the buildings but the main house washed away, the beach greatly damaged....A tree fell across one of the houses occupied by a family, and the occupants among which were two women who had to wade in water up to their chins to a place of safety. The houses were lodged against a woods two or three hundred yards distant....Thomas Maloney says that the big tidal wave came rolling in like a low cloud ten or twelve feet high and broke over the Island just before sun up.

The grand resort at Woodland Beach was never rebuilt, and today the only tangible evidence of its existence is a set of old pilings from the destroyed boardwalk, which are sometimes visible at low tide. However, a small community still survives along the bay at Woodland Beach. The beach itself is unguarded, so it is not recommended to walk it at night. In

A partial view of the Woodland Beach community in 2020.

Woodland Beach at sunset.

the present day, a steel fishing pier extends from the shore far out onto the water. As I stood there in the rain in the summer of 2020, I was struck by how violent the water was and how the strong winds chilled me to the bone. How vulnerable I felt in such a beautiful place.

When the sun goes down, electric lights illuminate the pier for those who are interested in night fishing. Many people who have stood on the Woodland Beach pier at night have reported experiencing strange things, especially in the month of October as Halloween creeps closer. Witnesses have reported hearing the sounds of many people talking and laughing suddenly penetrating the silence. Turning toward the sounds, sometimes people have seen the lost boardwalk of Woodland Beach appear in the mist just as it looked back in the nineteenth century, filled with people dressed in clothing from another time. It is said that near the anniversary of the great tidal wave of 1878, the souls of all those who lost their lives in the disaster return to Woodland Beach and are visible for a few moments before they vanish back into history.

As my partner and I drove away from Woodland Beach on the single road that barely rises above the marshland, we soon saw the road was now flooded much worse than before. We had no choice but to try to get through it or stay the night at a haunted beach where dozens of people drowned. We drove slowly, it continued to rain and the water continued to rise. Suddenly, our car stopped in the middle of this river, and the engine went dead. And I felt deeply afraid. I swear I could almost hear a ghostly voice whispering to me from outside the car window, low and rasping, filled with water:

"You see? This fear? This dread? This…this is what it felt like."

Then the car started up again, and we drove slowly through the dark water up to the safety of the mainland.

9

THE SKULL IN THE SCARLET HATBOX

Old Patty Cannon
Is dead and gone
Can't you hear the devil
Draggin' her along?

That is an old nursery rhyme that was common in Sussex County over a century ago, but it has faded from memory now. The same may be said to some degree for its subject, Patty Cannon. Although she was one of the most notorious women of the early nineteenth century and may have been one of the first female serial killers in the United States, the gruesome and horrific tale of her life and crimes is not as well known as one would expect. Perhaps that is understandable. We often sweep the most unsavory aspects of our history under the rug, hoping they will eventually be forgotten.

Despite the fact that the Seaford Historical Society's museum, located in the town I was born in, has an exhibit about her, and the fact that I was raised in Georgetown, which is where Patty Cannon's violent life met a suitably violent end, I had not heard of Patty Cannon until about a year ago. In all the lessons about Delaware and Sussex County history I had throughout grade school, she was never mentioned. It was only when I happened to be talking with my mother about writing this book that she said I should tell the tale of Patty Cannon, who was buried near the jail in Georgetown, a place I had driven past hundreds of times in my youth. So, I began to do research on Patty Cannon, and what I discovered was a dark corner of Delaware's history I had not been aware of before. But it needs to be remembered.

Much of Patty Cannon's early life is shrouded in mystery, and even nearly two hundred years after her death, so much of who she was remains a tantalizing question mark. No letters she wrote during her lifetime have survived, but given that she made her considerable fortune illegally, perhaps this is not surprising. She, and the others involved with her hellish gang, covered their tracks well. It was only when she was an old woman that she was finally arrested, and even that came about because of a fortunate accident. The primary sources we have are mostly newspaper articles quoting witnesses, as well as her indictment, which is preserved in the Delaware Public Archives. There are numerous secondary sources that were written in the decades following her death purporting to tell the whole story, but in them the truth was already becoming mixed with legend. The legend of Patty Cannon has only continued to grow.

Two books have done heroic work in separating the truth of Patty Cannon from the myth that has sprung up around her. In 1998, Hal Roth published *The Monster's Handsome Face: Patty Cannon in Fiction and Fact*, a book that has a plain black cover imprinted with the white image of her skull. I had often seen it on bookstore shelves when I was growing up, but I never picked it up because the cover frightened me. Michael Morgan's 2015 book *Delmarva's Patty Cannon: The Devil on the Nanticoke* also does a fantastic job of helping the reader understand the historical context of the times in which Patty committed her atrocities. I recommend both books to anyone who wishes to get a fuller account than I have room for here.

———◆———

PATTY CANNON WAS BORN sometime between 1759 and 1769. Some historians believe she may have immigrated to the United States from Canada, but we cannot know for sure. The first thing that is certain about Patty is that in 1790 she married a farmer named Jesse Cannon, and they settled near a town that was then known as Johnson's Crossroads, named for the tavern run by Joe Johnson. This community was on the borders of Sussex County, Delaware, and Maryland's Caroline and Dorchester Counties, a mix of jurisdictions that Patty, Jesse Cannon, Joe Johnson and their gang would use to great advantage in the decades to come. It was incredibly easy for them to slip between one state and another, especially then, using the dense forests and the Nanticoke River to escape detection.

We know that Patty and Jesse Cannon had a least one daughter whose name has been lost to history. This daughter eventually married Joe Johnson and happily entered the family business, sharing her mother's love of sadism. Patty Cannon herself was described by those who knew her as a heavy woman who possessed enormous physical strength, often disguising herself as a man while committing her misdeeds. She had black eyes and long, lustrous black hair; loved dancing and music; and was regarded as an engaging and witty hostess to those who happened to stop by the tavern at Johnson's Crossroads. Many of the men carrying large sums of dollars and gold who had a few drinks with Patty Cannon never left the tavern alive.

A woman named June Truitt, interviewed by Hal Roth for his book *The Monster's Handsome Face*, related a chilling anecdote that had been passed down by the old-timers of Sussex County:

> *A man from Federalsburg was going to Seaford one day with some meat to sell to a butcher. On his way he stopped at the tavern…and Patty said to him, "On your way back, stop again." I guess she thought he'd have some money with him then. Coming back, he went all the way around on another route; he was so scared of her.*

Patty Cannon was indeed a person to be feared. She was the undisputed leader of the Cannon-Johnson gang for decades, and the terrible business they were primarily engaged in was kidnapping both free and enslaved Black people and selling them South, an Underground Railroad in reverse. In an age when you could buy an acre of land for one dollar, a young and healthy Black man could be sold South for three hundred. In this way, Patty Cannon and her gang made many thousands of dollars while causing unimaginable human misery, striking fear into the hearts of Black men, women and children throughout Delaware, Maryland and Pennsylvania. Michael Morgan writes in his book *Delmarva's Patty Cannon*:

> *Inviting targets could be abducted and transported to Patty Cannon's house, which was on the border between Delaware and Maryland….The second story of Patty's house contained two rooms that were not connected. Each of these rooms formed a cell that was accessible by a separate staircase. The unique arrangement of these two rooms made them ideal for holding kidnap victims….Those around Patty were a loose collection of malcontents who came and went as they were arrested, killed, or moved on to other dubious ventures. Joe Johnson, an experienced kidnapper, was physically*

intimidating, six foot tall, mean and fearless. Johnson maintained a tavern...situated a short distance from Patty's house....With easy access to the Nanticoke River, the victims collected at Patty's house could be added to those at the tavern and shipped down the river to Southern parts, where they could be sold for handsome profits.

Held in attics and basements for weeks at a time, chained, brutalized and nearly starved, these kidnapped Black people would then be forcibly marched in leg irons through miles of dense forest to reach the river. Whenever someone would cry out in pain or begin to slow down with exhaustion, Patty and Joe Johnson were known to viciously whip their victims into submission. Patty's daughter, married to Joe Johnson, would often accompany them, and is reported to have said that "it did her good to see him beat the boys." She was truly her mother's daughter.

It became known throughout the local community and far beyond what the Cannon-Johnson gang members were doing, but for many years they evaded capture. Patty Cannon learned early that dead men, and dead women, and dead children, tell no tales. And after all, most of her victims were Black. There were many locals who were perfectly willing to allow Patty's work to continue. However, there were some who tried to stop it. An abolitionist named Jesse Torrey, who investigated the kidnappings, said the members of this nefarious gang were like "beasts of prey...extending their ravages, generally attended with bloodshed and sometimes murder, and spreading terror and consternation amongst both Freemen and slaves throughout the sandy regions from the western to the eastern shores."

Finally, in July 1821, Joe Johnson was arrested for kidnapping. This marked the first time the law was able to touch Patty Cannon's gang, although she was not charged. The police procured a warrant to search Johnson's tavern for three kidnapped Black men. They found the three they were seeking, along with ten others. An article in Maryland's *Eastern Gazette* related the story, including the names and ages of the thirteen Black men and children who were found in captivity at Joe Johnson's tavern for the purpose of being illegally sold South:

1. Samuel Carlisle, aged about fifty-five.
2 & 3. Nocre and Isaac Griffith, the first aged about nine, and the other about four.
4. Lowel Thorpe, aged twenty-three years.

5 & 6. Jacob and Spencer Francis, the first aged twenty and the other nineteen years, are brothers, free born.
7. Jacob Eveson, aged seventeen years...free born.
8. George Williams, aged nineteen years...free born.
9. John Todd, aged eleven years...free born.
10. James Morris, aged sixteen...free born.
11. George Morgan, aged fifteen...free born.
12. John Dominick, aged about ten years.
13. Henry Ingram, aged about thirteen years.
Those persons are now in Georgetown where their friends may make application for them.

This is only one example of a group of Black people Patty Cannon and her gang were planning to sell South. If successful, these thirteen people would have been sold for almost $4,000. There were countless other Black men, women and children successfully sold South by Patty's gang over the decades in batches just like this one, whose names and lives are now unknown and lost to time.

Joe Johnson was convicted of his kidnapping charges and sentenced to thirty-nine lashes in the public pillory and then to have the soft parts of his ears cut off, as was customary in the law of the time. The lashes were given to him, and as many as two thousand spectators came to watch, as they did every time a public whipping occurred. The soft parts of Joe Johnson's ears were not cut off, however; that aspect of his sentence was commuted by the governor. This close call with the law did not stop Joe Johnson, Patty, Jesse Cannon and the other members of the gang from continuing their atrocious work.

Five years later, around 1826, Patty's husband, Jesse Cannon, died. Some say that she poisoned him. After this, Patty Cannon seems to have slowed down. She was getting older, no longer strong enough to subdue a man by herself as she had once been able to do. Over her many years of crimes, Patty had amassed a great deal of money. But, in her last few years, she began to visit the homes of wealthy Maryland and Delaware families, telling fortunes for supplemental income. For all intents and purposes, with all the evil things she had done in her lifetime, it looked like Patty Cannon was going to get away with all of it in the end, likely to die peacefully in her bed without ever facing justice.

However, old Patty Cannon happened to lease her land to a tenant farmer, an action that would at last prove her undoing on April 1, 1829, finally unmasking her true, monstrous face to the entire world. An April 1829 article in the *Delaware Gazette* tells the harrowing tale:

About ten days previous to this writing, a tenant, who lives on the farm where Patty Cannon and her son-in-law, the celebrated Joseph Johnson, Negro trader lived…was ploughing a field in a place where a heap of brush had been laying for years, when his horse sunk in a grave, and on digging he found a blue painted chest, about three feet long, and in it were found the bones of a man.…

The excitement produced by the discovery, as may naturally be supposed, was very great in the neighborhood, and on [April 2] one of Johnson's gang, named Cyrus James, who has resided in Maryland, was caught in this state, and brought before a justice of the peace in Seaford, and on examination said that…Patty Cannon had shot the man while at supper in her house, and that he saw [her] engaged in carrying him in the chest and burying him: and stated moreover that many others had been killed, and that he could show where they had been buried.…

In one place, a garden, they dug and found the bones of a young child, the mother of which, he stated, was a Negro woman belonging to Patty Cannon, which child, being a Mulatto, she had killed for the reason she supposed its father to be one of her own family. Another place a few feet distant was then pointed out, when, upon digging a few feet two oak boxes were found, each of which contained human bones.

Those in one of them had been of a person about seven years of age, which James said he saw Patty Cannon knock in the head with a billet of wood, and the other contained those of one whom he said they considered bad property; by which, it is supposed they meant that he was Free.…On examining the skull of the largest child, it was discovered to be broken as described by James.

The fellow James was raised by Patty Cannon, having been bound to her at the age of seven years, and is said to have done much mischief in his time for her and Johnson.…This woman is now between sixty and seventy years of age, and looks more like a man than a woman; but old as she is, she is believed to be as heedless and heartless as the most abandoned wretch that lives.

Patty Cannon has been lodged in the jail at Georgetown.…James stated that he had not shown all the places where murdered bodies had been buried, and at the time of writing, our correspondent informs us, the people were still digging…The neighborhood in which these terrible events

NARRATIVE AND CONFESSIONS.

OF

LUCRETIA P. CANNON,

WHO WAS TRIED, CONVICTED, AND SENTENCED TO BE
HUNG AT GEORGETOWN, DELAWARE, WITH
TWO OF HER ACCOMPLICES.

CONTAINING

AN ACCOUNT OF SOME OF THE MOST HORRIBLE AND SHOCKING MURDERS
AND DARING ROBBERIES EVER COMMITTED BY ONE OF THE FEMALE SEX.

Page 16.

NEW YORK:

PRINTED FOR THE PUBLISHERS

1841.

Title page of the *Narrative and Confessions of Lucretia P. Cannon*, 1841. Public domain.

occurred, the borders of Delaware and Maryland, have long been famous for Negro stealing and Negro trading—and Patty Cannon and Joe Johnson are familiar names to us.

Familiar names to them for nearly thirty years. They knew what was happening and did not stop it. It is said that the town newspaper crier called throughout the streets of Seaford, Delaware, on the day the monster was at last arrested: "Three o'clock! And Patty Cannon's taken!"

Patty Cannon was indicted on four counts of murder. She likely killed dozens more than that, but these were the bones that were found. Patty was, in a just turn, now locked in a cell of her own, a prisoner whose trial was set to be one of the highlights of the early nineteenth century.

On May 11, 1829, Patty Cannon was found dead in her jail cell. She was between sixty and seventy years old. The cause of her death is not recorded in the primary sources that still survive, which seems unusual for so notorious a criminal. However, one clue comes from a letter written by Senator John Clayton, who had been a part of the trial of Joe Johnson in 1822. Clayton wrote in 1837, eight years after Patty Cannon's jailhouse death, "This demon took arsenic and died by her own hand." The total truth of how Patty Cannon died in her cell will likely never be known. But it is known her corpse was buried in an unmarked grave near the Georgetown jailhouse.

In 1841, twelve years after Patty Cannon died, an American penny dreadful was published under the title *Narrative and Confessions of Lucretia P. Cannon: The Female Murderer.* This work is responsible for the confusion that "Lucretia" was Patty Cannon's true first name. This is false. The writers likely hoped to link Patty Cannon with the historical figure of Italy's Lucrezia Borgia, who is often interpreted as a brilliant murderer. Here is how this penny dreadful begins:

> *It has probably never fallen to the lot of man to record a list of more cruel, heart-rending, atrocious, cold-blooded, and horrible crimes and murders than have been perpetuated by the subjects of this narrative...deeds too, which for the depravity of every human feeling, seems to have scarcely found a parallel in the annals of crime. And it seems doubly shocking, and atrocious, when we find them committed by one of the female sex.*

The *Narrative and Confessions of Lucretia P. Cannon* of 1841 includes an atrocity not mentioned in Cyril James's testimony, one that has become an integral part of Patty Cannon's legend:

On one occasion, one of the Negro women had a little child about five years old sometimes subject to fits, and in these fits the child used to scream in a terrible manner. It happening to have one of these fits while in Lucretia Cannon's house, she became so enraged upon hearing its cries, that she flew at the child, tearing the clothes from off the poor victim of her wrath, beating it at the same time in a dreadful manner; and, as if this was not enough to satisfy her more than brutal disposition, she caught it up and held its face to a hot fire, and thus scorched the child to death in her own hands, burning its face to a cinder. She then threw it in the cave in the cellar.

It could have happened.

---◆---

THE TRUTH OF PATTY Cannon became further mixed up with legend with the publication of George Alfred Townsend's wildly bestselling 1884 historical novel *The Entailed Hat, or Patty Cannon's Crimes.* Townsend was what we might call one of the first investigative journalists in the United States, notably covering the assassination of Abraham Lincoln and its aftermath. In writing about Patty Cannon and her atrocities, he wove a sensational tale that is also based on interviews he conducted with locals who had known the perpetrators involved. Townsend's *The Entailed Hat* remains a fascinating blend of true facts and fiction. I quote the following passages below because they *might* give a fleeting glimpse into Patty Cannon's character. First, we go back to her glory days as the deadly mistress of the tavern at Johnson's Crossroads:

McLane went to his portmanteau and unlocked it and took out rolls of banknotes and a buckskin bag of gold. The yellow luster seemed to flash in Patty Cannon's rich black eyes, like the moon overhead upon a well. "How beautiful it do shine, Cunnil!" she said. "Nothing is like it fur a friend. Youth an' beauty has got to go together to be strong, but, by God! Gold kin go it alone."

As he made one step to penetrate the darkness with his dazzled eyes, Patty Cannon silently thrust against his heart a huge horse-pistol and pulled the trigger: a flash of fire from the sharp flint against the pan lit up the hall in an instant, and the heavy body of the guest fell backward before his chair, and over him leaned the woman a moment, still as death....He did not move, but only bled at the large lips, ghastly and unprotesting, and the cold blue eyes looked as natural as life.

Patty Cannon took the chair and counted the money.

The Entailed Hat also gives Patty Cannon a phantasmagoric visitation before her death in jail reminiscent of a diabolical version of Charles Dickens's ghostly *Christmas Carol*:

Sleeping in her chains, there were children's eyes watching her from far off corners, as if to say, "Give us the whole life we would have lived but for you!" As her swollen limbs festered to the irons, there were babies' cries floating in the air, that seemed to draw near her breasts, as if for food, and suddenly convulsed there in screams of pain, and move away with the sounds of suffocation....All night there were callers on her, and whom they were no one could tell: but the jailer's family saw her lips moving and her eyes consult the air....But suddenly a helpless something would appear, and paralyze her with its little wail, like a babeless mother or a motherless babe, and, with her forehead wet with sweat of agony, she would affect to chuckle, and would whisper, "Nothin' but n----rs! Nothin' more!" That night... Patty Cannon, the murderess...died in awful torments.

Of course, all this is merely fiction. In reality, it is likely she felt no remorse at all and would rather die alone by her own hand than face justice for her heinous, racist crimes against humanity. With all her fearsome reputation in life, Patty Cannon died a coward. Patty Cannon's mysterious death was recorded in the newspapers of May 11, 1829, as a vague postscript, and her body was buried in an unmarked grave near the Georgetown jail.

------◆------

IN 1961, THE DOVER Public Library received an unusual bequest. It was a scarlet hatbox, and inside the hatbox, nestled on a pillow of red velvet, there was a human skull over one hundred years old. Documents were also included in the hatbox, and this is what they said:

PATTY CANNON'S SKULL

Just after the turn of the century, James Marsh (my uncle by marriage) was reading law....He took the position of deputy sheriff of Sussex County. While holding this job the bodies of Patty Cannon and one or two others who had been buried in the jail yard of the Sussex Jail were exhumed for reburial in potter's field. The yard now is a parking lot....Somehow while moving these bodies Patty's skull came into the possession of James Marsh.

About 1907, James Marsh contracted acute tuberculosis and, in an effort to save himself, moved to Denver, Colorado. At this time, he gave the skull to my father, Charles I. Joseph of Angola, Sussex County, for keeping. From that time until the late thirties the skull hung on a nail in a rafter of my father's barn, by which time it had become quite a curiosity. To save it from damage or possible theft he put it in a box and stored it in the attic of his home. At his death in 1946 I took possession of the skull and in 1961 put it on loan to the Dover Library.

—Alfred W. Joseph
Dover, Delaware
May 2, 1963

For decades, the skull of Patty Cannon sat in a scarlet hatbox in a locked room of the Dover Library, only shown to the brave mortals who asked to see it. The skull of Patty Cannon was donated to the Smithsonian Museum of Washington, D.C., in 2010. They believe it is authentic.

———◆———

PATTY CANNON'S HOUSE WAS demolished soon after World War II, and only one photograph of it is known to survive. Today, a historical marker notes where her house was once. Joe Johnson's tavern is also long gone now, and the town of Johnson's Crossroads, situated on the border between Delaware and Maryland, was eventually renamed Reliance. Cannon's Ferry, operated by one of Patty's relatives who had nothing to do with murders, changed its name to the Woodland Ferry, which is still operating daily in the twenty-first century.

In 2012, the Delaware Public Archives erected another historical marker in the town of Seaford, Delaware. It bears the title THE CANNON/JOHNSON KIDNAPPING GANG, and the text of the marker reads:

In the early 1800s the headquarters of the notorious Cannon/Johnson Kidnapping Gang was located close to this site. After the importation of African slaves was legally outlawed in 1808, demand for slave labor in the expanding states of the Deep South continued to grow. The Cannon/Johnson Gang specialized in the criminal kidnapping of free African-Americans for sale into slavery. Through their secret network that stretched as far south as Alabama and Mississippi, it is believed they abducted hundreds of persons of color and sold them into slavery. Establishing their headquarters in three different counties along this boundary of Delaware & Maryland, the gang managed to avoid arrest by local government officials. Authorities only took substantial action against the gang after they discovered evidence of the murder of a white slave trader and the bodies of several others, including a young child and a baby. Most of the gang escaped to the Deep South, except for Patty Cannon, who was captured and imprisoned in the Sussex County jail. Although controversy surrounds the way she died in May 1829, it is believed that Cannon committed suicide while awaiting trial for murder. This memorial is dedicated to the victims of this evil enterprise, and those who struggled against it.

No matter what may be attempted to erase the terrible truth of the past, reminders of Patty Cannon's long reign of terror still haunt Delaware in the present. She is the demon woman's skull in the scarlet hatbox. She is one of the First State's most horrifying real human monsters.

10

A HAUNTED HISTORY OF LEWES

I could not possibly describe the town of Lewes better than the Federal Writers' Project did in their 1938 book, *Delaware: A Guide to the First State*:

> *Lewes...the saltiest town in Delaware, is known to every ship captain who has ever picked up a pilot for the river, or has ever rounded Cape Henlopen in a gale to find shelter behind the Delaware Breakwater. As the home of Delaware pilots for at least 280 years, Lewes ("Lewestown" to older residents) has a tradition of the sea borne by every east wind that haunts its narrow streets and aged cypress-shingled houses. Its present is saturated in the drama of its past. There is a Fountain of Youth on Pilot Town Road, a Ship Carpenter Street, a Knitting Street, and a Frog Alley. Lewes has been plundered by privateers and has bargained with Captain Kidd for his loot; it has been bombarded in war and knows all about shipwreck and sunken treasure. Because of the Dutch settlement here in 1631, Lewes is to Delaware what Plymouth is to Massachusetts and Jamestown is to Virginia. It has been a seat of Colonial and county government under four flags, and its residents have had much to do in the making of Delaware history.*

No matter where you go in the town of Lewes, you are surrounded by history. When I was a child walking around the historic district near the riverfront, I would imagine that I was in the town of Collinsport, Maine, the supernaturally infested fictional setting of the 1960s television soap opera *Dark Shadows*. That's not far from the truth. Lewes has always had a connection to the sea, and because of its rich and often turbulent past, it also has many tales of the unexplained that continue to echo in the present.

Since before recorded history, the area now known as Lewes, Delaware, was the home of the Siconese Native tribes, who are sometimes also grouped with the Nanticoke and Lenape people. The first White European colony was established by the Dutch on June 3, 1631, after they "purchased" the land from the Native people who had lived there for perhaps thousands of years. They named their settlement Swanendael, meaning "Valley of the Swans." In the modern era, the spelling has been amended to Zwaanendael, but that spelling never appeared on any documents from the colonial period. The Dutch built a fort and dwellings for the colony's thirty-two inhabitants and began to farm the land as well as engaging in whaling. A man named David de Vries was one of the leaders of the Swanendael colony but was not among the original settlers. The decision not to accompany them to the colony in 1631 saved his life.

In 1632, less than a year after the establishment of the Swanendael colony, David de Vries received news that the colony had been massacred by the Native tribes. On December 2, 1632, de Vries arrived and saw the signs of slaughter for himself. The fort had been burned, and de Vries wrote in an anguished letter home that on investigating the Swanendael site he had "found lying here and there the skulls and bones of our people and the heads of the horses and cows which they had brought with them." Only one colonist, Thunus Willemsen, had somehow survived. The other thirty-one members of the Dutch Swanendael colony were dead, their remains rotting in the sun, filling the air around the site with the sickly sweet perfume of their decaying human flesh.

Daniel de Vries immediately tried to find out how things could have gone so wrong at the Swanendael colony. His testimony is the only primary source we have for what happened, and it is important to take it with a grain of salt. The narrative that follows conveniently casts the White European colonists as "good" and "civilized," while the Native American tribes are depicted as being "violent" and "savage," a racial stereotype we know is false. The story told by David de Vries is the one that has entered the historical record as true. I suspect that if we had the Native side of the tale not filtered through a White lens, the story might be different. Or perhaps not.

In his excellent book *Hidden History of Lewes*, author Michael Morgan describes the genesis and bloody execution of the Swanendael massacre like this:

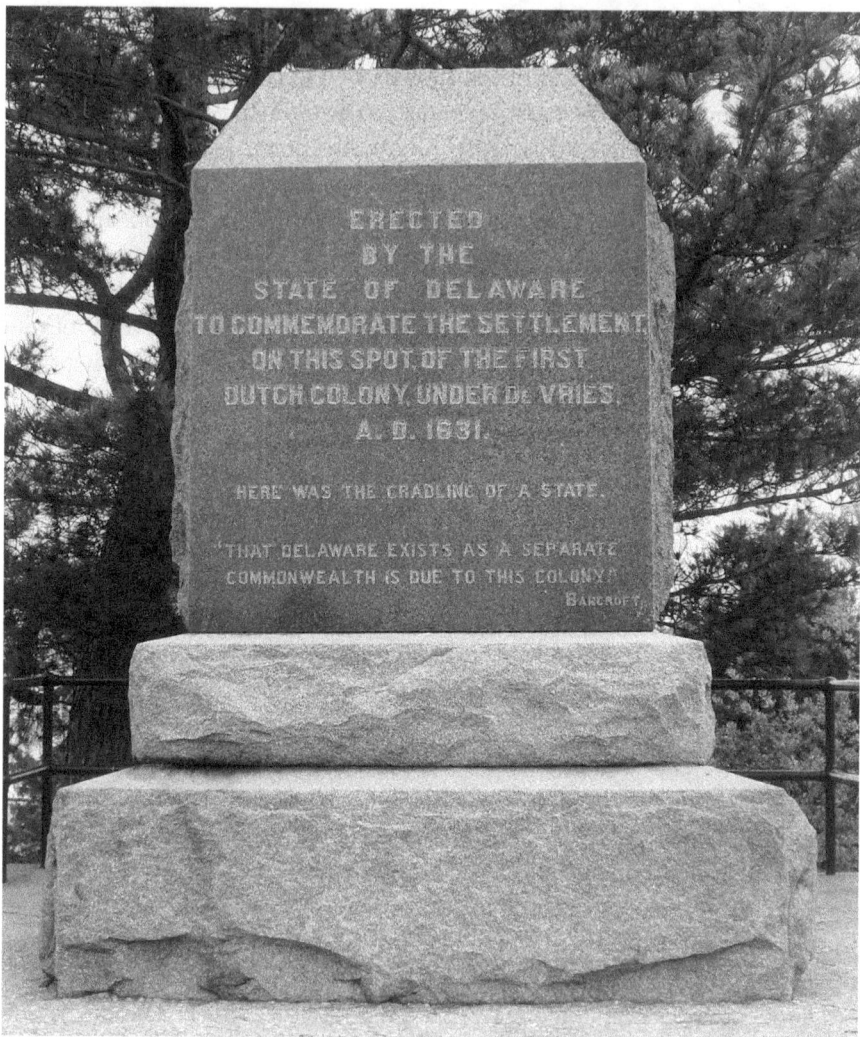

Monument of the site of the Swanendael Colony. *Photograph by The Red Hat of Pat Ferrick, public domain.*

A Native American showed de Vries the place where the Swanendael settlers had set up a pole to which they attached a piece of tin painted with the coat of arms of Holland. The Native American told de Vries that one of the Siconese had innocently taken the tin to make a pipe for tobacco, upsetting the Dutch settlers. When the colonists complained to the Siconese, the Native American said, "They went away and slew the Chief who had done it and brought a token of the dead to the house of those in command, who told them that they wished they had not done it...." After this scolding from the Dutch colonists, the incident further escalated. The Native American told de Vries, "They then went away, and the friends of the murdered Chief incited their friends...to set about the work of revenge." A few days later, several Siconese arrived at Swanendael with a number of beaver skins to trade with the Dutch settlers. Having gained entrance to the fort, the disgruntled Native Americans attacked and killed all the settlers of Swanendael.

The exact location of the Swanendael colony is not definitively known, and there are several historical plaques located throughout the town of Lewes that commemorate the site. In 1931, on the three-hundred-year anniversary of the settlement, the Zwaanendael Museum was opened in Lewes, and it remains open today as a must-visit cultural institution dedicated to preserving and interpreting Delaware's early history. A history that, whether we like it or not, was born in blood.

Subsequently, other Dutch and Mennonite settlements sprang up near the site of the Swanendael massacre, and the region became known as Whorekill. *Kill* is Dutch for "river." For example, the Schuylkill River

The Zwaanendael Museum. *Photograph by SmallBones, public domain.*

that flows through Philadelphia means "Hidden River," but the Delaware equivalent leaves little room for interpretation. Historical tradition says that the Native Siconese/Lenape tribes had a tradition of "sharing" their women with the male Dutch settlers, who then gallantly decided to give the river and the region the name of Whorekill. It is not surprising that, in 1682, when William Penn was granted "the three counties on the Delaware" as part of his enormous land gift from the King of England, that one of Penn's first written priorities was to find a name to replace Whorekill. The name chosen was Lewes, and the rest, as they say, is history.

———•———

THE TOWN OF LEWES is notorious for its many yarns of deadly shipwrecks, sunken treasures and ghostly galleons, but perhaps the most famous of these stories is the tale of the *De Braak*.

The HMS *De Braak* was a vessel captained by a man by the name of James Drew, who possessed a fearsome reputation. During the Battle of Bunker Hill in 1775, British soldier James Drew committed what was even then described as "atrocities." After the battle had ended, he went through the field of corpses of American Patriots, shooting any he found still alive. Upon finding the shallow grave of a particular rival named Dr. Joseph Warren, Drew dug up Warren's rotting corpse, spit on it, stomped on the body and then cut off its head.

In May 1798, James Drew found himself captain of the *De Braak*, sailing near Cape Henlopen in Lewes, Delaware. The ship was reportedly carrying a large amount of treasure pillaged from Spanish ships, including copper, cocoa and, most importantly, gold and silver, valued at many millions of dollars. Captain James Drew was feeling satisfied with his work as he approached the Delaware shore, so much so that he paid little attention to the dark and fearsome storm clouds gathering above his ship.

Within minutes of the storm breaking directly above the *De Braak*, it was obvious the ship was doomed to sink to the bottom of the ocean. The wind and the rain lashed the vessel until it capsized, taking most of its crew, including Captain James Drew and all its treasure, hurtling down to the bottom of the sea near Lewes beach. In total, forty-seven sailors lost their lives. Some bodies, including Captain Drew's, washed up on shore. Many more rest in the vast graveyard that is the sea near Cape Henlopen.

Many have sought to retrieve the treasure rumored to have been lost in the tragic wreck of the *De Braak*. One of the most notable was a man named

Charles N. Costad, who in 1935 said to the press, "We have been encouraged in what we have accomplished and believe we are on the right trail." But then the dark clouds, along with vicious wind and ferocious thunder and lightning, returned. Costard and his crew were unable to do any diving for the lost *De Braak* treasure due to the intense storm. They began to believe that the storm was created by a supernatural force tasked with protecting the cursed treasure, and they called it the Bad Weather Witch.

Michael Morgan wrote of this incident in an October 2016 article for DelmarvaNow.com:

The superstitious sailors decided on an elaborate ritual to exorcise the evil spirit. After the demon was drawn on cardboard, the treasure hunters then used the cardboard image for target practice. After the first attempt to drive the Weather Witch away failed, the sailors constructed an effigy of the Weather Witch. The old hag had long gray hair that streamed from under a tall peaked cap. Equipped with a broomstick and clothed with a flowing cape, the witch was given the position of honor in the cabin, offered drink and food, and then was burned, with many incantations, in the galley stove. At sunset, the witch's ashes were collected and scattered on the sea. The sailors' exorcism appeared to have angered the Sea Witch. Strong winds whipped the sea into high waves and made the salvage vessels unmanageable....Defeated by the demon of the deep, Colstad abandoned the search for the De Braak.

The wreck of the *De Braak* was finally raised from its sea grave off Cape Henlopen in 1986, and many of its artifacts are on display in the Zwaanendael Museum. Significantly, none of the treasure associated with the ship has ever been found. Since 1989, the Sea Witch Festival of Sussex County has honored the legend of the Bad Weather Witch, becoming one of the most popular Halloween festivals in all of Delaware.

Also, the *De Braak* has become a literal ghost ship, seen by many sailors on the water since its tragic sinking in 1798. Like the legendary *Flying Dutchman*, the *De Braak* has been seen appearing on the sea near where it was wrecked at Cape Henlopen on dark, stormy, foggy nights. Those who have seen this ghostly vessel have reported it is operated by a crew of decomposing, waterlogged human skeletons, with its undead captain, James Drew, hanging from the mast by his broken neck. Witnesses then watch in horror as the phantom ship slowly begins its descent into the icy, unforgiving ocean, hearing the cracking of its timbers and the agonizing screams of its crew, doomed to re-enact their watery deaths for all eternity. The specter of Captain James Drew has also been seen haunting his grave at St. Peter's Church in downtown Lewes, rising from his tomb to search for the lost treasure.

———◆———

DURING THE WAR OF 1812, the town of Lewes was bombarded by British cannonballs. The cannons Delawareans used to successfully fight back against the British during that time are still visible in Memorial Park, and there is a single cannonball embedded in a simple house near the water. It is only for show, but the Cannonball House, built in 1765 and now the home of the Lewes Historical Society, is one of the town's haunted houses where there is a recorded tragic death. But it's not because of the besiegement of the War of 1812. The Cannonball House on Front Street is haunted due to the grisly death of Susan Rowland King, over one hundred years later.

Susan Rowland King lived in what is now called the Cannonball House in 1917. She was a widow, twice over, living alone in this old dark house. After a long and hard day's work, on March 20, 1917, Susan, who owned her home, poured herself a big glass of wine and sat by the fireplace. A huge gust of wind came in from the open window, causing the flames from the fireplace to blow outward and ignite her dress. Susan was on fire. She screamed and she screamed and she screamed again until a neighbor finally found Susan writhing in her bed, her entire body burned almost beyond recognition. Susan did not die of her agonizing injuries inside the Cannonball House but mercifully succumbed to sweet death in a nearby hospital a few days later.

However, it is said that ever since her grisly passing, Susan Rowland King's ghost has haunted the rooms of the Cannonball House. A subsequent owner of the house once nailed the door to what had been Susan's bedroom shut. He returned a few days later to find the bedroom door wide open and the nails laid neatly side by side on the floor. No matter what subsequent occupants have done to close that door, it somehow always opens all by itself. Over the years, many have also heard the sound of footsteps in the house. When they go to investigate, no one is ever found. Several members of the Lewes Historical Society interviewed over the years have stated that they refused to be left to work in the Cannonball House alone. They feel "uncomfortable" there. They will not say why.

Another haunted home in Lewes is the Ryves Holt House. Constructed in 1665, it is the oldest surviving building in the state of Delaware. First built to serve as an inn, it was purchased by in 1721 by Ryves Holt, the first chief justice of Sussex County. Like the nearby Cannonball House, it is now owned by the Lewes Historical Society. Also like the Cannonball House, the Ryves Holt House is haunted by the ghost of a woman named Susan.

In 1683, the battered body of Susan Johnson was discovered dead at the bottom of the stairs in her home. Her husband, John Johnson, was suspected by many in Lewes of beating and finally murdering his wife, and he was soon arrested and brought to trial. However, this trial was to be highly unusual for the seventeenth century. The all-male jury felt it was improper for them to examine Susan Johnson's body themselves, so an unprecedented all-female jury was selected in their place. To put this extraordinary event into historical perspective, women were not legally allowed to be jurors in the United States until 1937, over 250 years later. These twelve female jurors gathered at the Ryves Holt House, then the local inn, where Susan Johnson's naked corpse was laid out on a table. Their task was to examine her body and determine if her death was accidental or homicide. They observed her broken neck from the fall down the stairs, as well as the bruises, both new and old, on her cold, white flesh. The women found that, based on the evidence before them, they could not prove beyond a reasonable doubt that Susan Johnson's death was murder. John Johnson was acquitted.

However, the ghost of Susan Johnson seems to disagree with this verdict. A 2019 article in the *Baltimore Sun* written by Mike Klingaman reports on a paranormal investigation that was done at the Ryves Holt House, led by Lewes Historical Society director of education Marcos Salaverria. The guests on the tour used a ghost box, which is said to pick up the voices of the dead (like the one I used at the Rockwood Mansion). One night in 2010, it seems that the people on the tour actually made contact with the ghost of Susan Johnson through the ghost box.

Salaverria said, "What they heard was one word, repeated three times: 'pushed...pushed...pushed.' I listened to the recording; it sounds like a snake's hiss, long and slurred with static, like 'pusssssshhhhed.'" It seems that John Johnson may have gotten away with murdering his wife, but Susan Johnson's ghost still refuses to be silenced, determined to set the record straight over three hundred years after her tragic demise.

———◦———

CAPE HENLOPEN STATE PARK is one of Delaware's riches, but it is also one of its most haunted locations. Some say it is the domain of the Henlopen

One of the World War II "ghost towers" at Cape Henlopen State Park. *Photograph by VitaleBaby, Creative Commons License.*

Devil, the sole offspring of the terrifying American cryptid known all over the world as the Jersey Devil. The legend goes that in 1735 in New Jersey, a woman named Jane Leeds gave birth to twelve children. Upon becoming pregnant again after birthing twelve babies, Jane Leeds screamed, while in labor for her thirteenth child on a dark and stormy night, "Let the devil take this one!"

Mother Leeds's thirteenth child was born. It was a creature with hooves, a goat's head, bat wings and a forked tail. Growling and screaming, it beat everyone with its tail before flying up the chimney and heading into the woods. This is the Jersey Devil, and the Pine Barrens of New Jersey have been its home ever since.

But some say the Jersey Devil flew into Delaware and mated with the local mammals, and now there is that hellish and unnatural cryptid offspring sometimes called the Henlopen Devil haunting your campsite in the dead of the night. Campers have often heard unearthly shrieks piercing the quiet night air and heard the flapping of enormous wings above their tents. Several reports have been made of people waking in the morning to find their tent has been circled overnight by strange, large, inhuman footprints that are unlike those of any known animal in the area.

Fort Miles is also one of the most haunted places to visit at Cape Henlopen State Park. The fort's construction began in 1938, and it was formally dedicated on June 3, 1941, to serve as Delaware's defense during World War II. Fort Miles was never required to fire its guns in aggression. Many fire control and observation towers were also built on the Delaware coast in preparation for the war. Most of these "Ghost Towers" from the Second World War are still standing, and at least one of them, Tower 12, located by the Great Dune in Cape Henlopen State Park, is haunted. Over the years, many visitors have taken photographs of Tower 12, only to later find the image of a man's face visible inside the tower's window. Tower 12's door is locked and sealed shut. Some who approach that tower have heard a man's gruff voice say loudly, "Go away" when there is no other living human around to speak. One of the World War II soldiers remains, guarding his tower.

In the parking lot on the Delaware side of the popular Cape May–Lewes ferry, there exists a historical plaque erected in the latter years of the twentieth century:

UNKNOWN SAILORS CEMETERY. Lewes has been a port-of-call and a harbor-of-refuge since the 17th century. For generations during the age of sail, a public burial ground in this immediate locality became the final resting place for hundreds of sailors who lost their lives and whose unidentified bodies were here cast ashore. In remembrance of those persons whose remains are sheltered on this shore, this memorial is placed. May they find eternal repose.

This is wishful thinking, because many visitors and employees have encountered the lost and wandering specters of the sailors whose corpses washed up on the Lewes shore so long ago, who were then buried anonymously in a mass grave now covered by a modern parking lot. Historians estimate that as many as eight hundred sailors are laid to rest here. Some say that on very dark, quiet nights, you can hear screams coming from the water, the souls of the dead sailors wailing at their tragic fate.

The haunting extends to the Cape May–Lewes ferry terminal itself, where dozens of workers on the night shift over the years have seen and heard things that have terrified them. Dark, shadowy human figures have been witnessed by the naked eye and also captured walking from room to room on security cameras. Doors open and close by themselves. Hand dryers in the bathrooms turn on when there is no living person there. Supplies fall off shelves as if an invisible hand had thrown them. The smell of pipe tobacco smoke sometimes permeates the air. One night shift worker at the terminal even felt the touch of a wet, freezing cold hand caress her right shoulder when she was working all alone in the middle of the night. Whatever it was, it left a wet handprint on her shirt. She left the terminal immediately and never returned.

———◆———

AN IMPORTANT ARTICLE ABOUT the true Fountain of Youth in Lewes, Delaware, was published in a local newspaper called the *Cape Gazette* on August 9, 2019. It read:

Many people don't know that Lewes has a Fountain of Youth. It sits on the canal side of the historic Maull House property at 536 Pilottown Road and is owned by the Colonel David Hall Chapter of the National Society of the Daughters of the American Revolution. The Maull family included patriots who served in the American Revolution and were longtime owners of the house, which was built in 1739. Legend has it that the Fountain of Youth in Lewes was discovered by the area's first Dutch colonists in 1631. The tiny gazebo that marks the fountain was built by the Lewes Chamber of Commerce in 1937. At one time, the fountain had a spiral conch shell cup that hung from the gazebo and was said to boost the waters' regenerative powers. The cup is now missing, but the spring is still producing water.

The Fountain of Youth in Lewes as seen in 2020. *Photograph by Jacob Glickman.*

I visited the Fountain of Youth in Lewes for the first time on a rainy day in the summer of 2020. My partner brought a glass vial with him. As we bent down over the well, he removed grass and leaves that had fallen into the spring until he revealed the clear water underneath. He filled the glass vial with the water. And then we both took a sip from it. It was the sweetest, freshest water I have ever tasted.

11

BUMPS IN THE NIGHT ON BETHANY BEACH

U nlike most of Delaware, historians and archaeologists have found little evidence of a Native American presence in the area now known as Bethany Beach. Most Native tribes settled north of what is now called the Indian River, and many suspect the river's inlet may have acted as a natural barrier to human habitation. It was not until the year 1900, the dawn of the twentieth century, that the land soon to become Bethany Beach was officially settled. In 1938, the Federal Writers' Project described the unique genesis of the town:

> *Bethany Beach is a small ocean resort of well-kept, comfortable summer cottages and boarding houses, with a short boardwalk extending along the beach front. The white sand beach is gently sloping, and the surf bathing and fishing are unexcelled on the Delaware coast....The place retains a good deal of the religious atmosphere of its beginnings at the turn of the century....In 1898 this site was picked out from others up and down the Atlantic Coast by several members of the Christian Church Disciples of Scranton, PA, who were appointed to select a spot for the summer activities of the Christian Missionary Society of Maryland, Delaware, and the District of Columbia. Later forming the Bethany Beach Improvement Company, this group agreed to purchase the land and develop it, and to provide transportation from the railroad to this isolated place.*

Today, in contrast to the sometimes much rowdier summer populations of neighboring Rehoboth Beach and Dewey Beach, Bethany Beach and Fenwick Island to the south call themselves with pride "The Quiet Resorts." As you drive down the Coastal Highway of Delaware's eastern shore, the traffic all but vanishes after passing through Rehoboth and Dewey Beaches. You pass over the Indian River Inlet bridge and then get a beautiful view of the tranquility of Delaware Seashore State Park on either side of you. Finally, as you pull into the quiet town of Bethany Beach, you can feel the peace and relaxation settling within you. But after the sun sets and the boardwalk closes, Bethany Beach is not always quiet. Sometimes, things from the past go bump in the night.

The Addy Sea, located on Ocean View Parkway in Bethany Beach, is a historic oceanfront inn that is one of the crown jewels of Delaware. Built in 1901, it has been standing on the precipice of the Atlantic Ocean for 120 years. For most of its existence, it has operated as a bed-and-breakfast with twelve rooms. Once you step through its elegantly carved front doors and into its spacious front parlor, you are immediately immersed in lovingly preserved Victorian splendor. The rooms all look much as they would have at the turn of the twentieth century, except air conditioners have been added in recent years. Only one room has a television. The walls are decorated with Victorian paintings and prints, along with photographs of the Addy Sea itself from various stages of its incredible history. Many of the ceilings are tin, the fireplace mantelpieces are marble, and the entire house is filled with exquisitely crafted antique ornaments and furniture. Most of the rooms have a view of the ocean and the beach from large windows, the wraparound porch is lined with rocking chairs and you can walk directly off the porch and onto the sand in seconds.

One of the original settlers of Bethany Beach was a man from Pittsburgh named John M. Addy. In 1901, he decided to build a house right on the ocean as a summer home for his family, which consisted of his wife, Jennie, and their children, Will, Charlie, Walter and Ann. John Addy was a plumber by profession, and so his house on the beach was the first in the area to have both indoor plumbing and its interiors illuminated by gaslight. Due to its location so close to the Atlantic Ocean, the Addy Sea was particularly vulnerable to violent storms. Harsh winds and beach erosion from rough waves came terrifyingly close to annihilating the Addy Sea in 1920 and 1927, causing the entire house to be physically moved at least twice until it settled at its current location. Because of this, the house sometimes has weird, crooked angles reminiscent of Shirley Jackson's *The*

The Addy Sea as it appeared in 1907. *Delaware Public Archives.*

Haunting of Hill House. Door frames are occasionally off-center with the doors themselves discreetly shaved so they are able to be closed, and some of the old wooden floors slant slightly. This all adds to the beguiling charm of this old house by the sea.

The first known death to have occurred at the property was a man named Kurtz Addy, a relative of the original family that built the house. The stories handed down paint Kurtz Addy as a somewhat wild man, prone to drinking and rapid mood swings. Sometime in the 1920s, Kurtz Addy went up onto the roof of the house in the middle of the night for reasons unknown. He fell from the roof to his death, either by losing his balance accidentally or perhaps jumping off intentionally to commit suicide. We don't know which is true, but ever since, people sleeping in what is now known as room 11 on the third floor have sometimes been woken up in the dead of night to the sound of heavy footsteps walking on the roof above their heads.

After the stock market crash of 1929, the Addy family was one of millions who suffered loss during the Great Depression. The second generation of the family began to rent the Addy Sea's rooms to visitors and tourists in 1935. In 1974, what was now the third generation of the Addy family approached neighbors Leroy and Frances Gravatte, saying they were planning to sell the Addy Sea. The Gravattes purchased the house and continued to restore it and run it as a bed-and-breakfast, and the Addy Sea remains under the Gravatte family's ownership to this day.

Frances Gravatte may have been the first person to publicly speak about the Addy Sea being haunted. She was interviewed extensively by David J. Seibold and Charles J. Adams III in their book *Ghost Stories of the Delaware Coast*. In it, Frances said:

> *Oh, yes, we certainly have ghosts in here....One thing that happened was very odd. We had just bought the place and our busboy was out swimming. I was in the closet downstairs cleaning hymnals out of it. The closet door slowly creaked shut behind me. Finally, the busboy came back and heard me banging from inside. He came to my rescue and asked me who locked me in there. I couldn't say, of course. But I think it might have been Kurtz.*

The unexplained scent of a mysterious woman's floral perfume has been detected on the second-floor hallway when the inn was empty. Disembodied voices have also been heard talking in parts of the house that should be vacant. But there are three rooms out of the twelve where paranormal activity has been reported most consistently over the years: rooms 1, 6 and 11. Frances Gravatte said this about strange occurrences in room 1:

> *One night, I was sleeping there in Room 1. At about four o'clock in the morning, an imitation oil lamp just fell on my face. Another time I walked in the room, and in the middle of the floor was a piece of brown-stained old newspaper. I picked it up, looked at it, and it was the newspaper obituary of Kurtz Addy!*

She had never seen the obituary before and had no idea where it had come from, or who (or what) had placed it there. Room 1 was also formerly the bedroom of John M. Addy, the man who built the house back in 1901. Addy had a copper bathtub he was extremely fond of, so much so that he brought it to the Addy Sea all the way from his house in Pittsburgh. There have also been tales of guests taking a bath in the tub being disturbed when it begins to be violently shaken by unseen hands. Perhaps the ghost of John Addy doesn't like sharing his bathroom with the living guests who come to visit his former home.

If you choose to stay in room 6, you may also experience something unearthly and unsettling. Visitors have sometimes heard the sound of eerie organ music being played in the room. No explanation has ever been found.

Frances Gravatte said, "My in-laws would like to sit up in Room 6 and listen to the organ play, and it really did."

Room 11 is supposed by some to be the most haunted room at the Addy Sea. In addition to the ghostly footsteps of Kurtz Addy heard on the roof, there is another phantom that inhabits this chamber overlooking the ocean. Frances Gravatte believed the room to be haunted by the ghost of a man named Paul Dulaney. Dulaney was a frequent repairman at the Addy Sea, often maintaining the cedar shingles on the roof. He did not die in the house but in Georgia after falling from a peach tree. However, Frances was adamant that his spirit had returned to take up permanent residence in room 11: "Oh, yes, we've seen his ghost up there, we really have. We've seen a figure on the bed. My granddaughter felt a cold hand touch her up there."

There is also an intriguing review of the Addy Sea on TripAdvisor from March 12, 2016, written by the user DebNBuzz about their experience in room 11:

> Our stay had a purpose, and we were not disappointed. If you are into hauntings, rm 11 is a must. It is the room that Captain Addy fell to his death from while trying to climb to the roof. Our experience included the jacuzzi [the shower] turning itself on and our phone powering off when we tried to record it. The hostess we spoke to says that both electricians and plumbers say there is no reason for this but yet it happens.

Naturally, when I traveled to the Addy Sea in the summer of 2020 to conduct research, room 11 is the one I chose to stay in overnight. When I checked in, I informed the manager on duty that I was writing this book, and she replied pleasantly but firmly, "We're not haunted. There are stories, things on the internet. We don't like to advertise it. I've slept in all these rooms

The Addy Sea as it appears today from the beach.

alone, and nothing has ever happened to me." I told her I was interested in the history as much as the hauntings, and I was happy to be staying the night in such an idyllic place.

That night, after exploring the shops along the boardwalk of Bethany, my partner and I decided to walk back to the Addy Sea along the beach itself. It was dark, and there was no one else on the shore. Still, as we walked, I got the feeling that we were not alone. I felt like there was something walking behind me, and I found myself starting to get really frightened. This was a dark, deserted beach after all. Who knows what could happen? Suddenly, my partner and I both stopped walking at the same time. He pointed ahead. Just a few feet in front of us, we saw things come from the ocean—like white lights swirling in the wind and then landing on the sand. There were about six of them. They were solid; they were not a reflection. I have never seen anything like them before. They were there for a few seconds, and then they were gone.

Later on, in my research, I found the Delaware legend of corpse lights, which are said to be the souls of sailors drowned at sea appearing on the beaches at night. I wonder if that's what we saw that night on Bethany Beach—the corpse lights. I don't know. But I'll never forget it.

After my partner and I watched the things fade away, I looked to my left and saw fiery torches on the beach. These were the electric lights guiding visitors from the beach to the front porch of the Addy Sea. We sat in the rocking chairs looking out at the ocean for a while and then went up to room 11. Before going to bed, I decided to unplug the nightlight in the bathroom so it would be completely dark in the room once the lights were off. I fell asleep that night listening to the ocean waves washing the shore and feeling the cool sea breeze through the open window.

Sometime in the middle of the night, I awoke and opened my eyes. I saw a gentle orange glow emanating from the bathroom to my right. I thought vaguely, "That's funny," and then closed my eyes and went back to sleep. When I woke up in the morning, I went to the bathroom and had a bit of a shock. The nightlight, shaped like a seashell, that I had unplugged before going to bed, was now plugged back in. That was the orange glow I had seen coming from the bathroom in the middle of the night. My partner said he hadn't touched it, nor had I. But someone, or something, had plugged it back in while we slept.

I didn't tell the manager about that when we came downstairs the next morning. I just said we'd had a very pleasant night's sleep, and after hearing that, she smiled and said proudly, "See? No ghosts!" Then I sat down to

The luxurious and inviting Dining Room at the Addy Sea.

perhaps the most delicious breakfast I have ever eaten in my life, served in the Addy Sea's elegant dining room. And then, sadly, it was time to go.

I must say I was a bit conflicted about including the Addy Sea in this book after my visit. I respect and understand the current owner's wish that the ghostly legends of its past not be promoted further—the Addy Sea has so many other great reasons for guests to visit. In the end, I decided to include it because previous owners have been so vocal in the past about the spookier side of the house's history and also because I think the Addy Sea Historic Oceanfront Inn is truly one of Delaware's hidden treasures that everyone should experience.

Perhaps the Addy Sea Inn is no longer haunted, like the manager said—but I understand why the ghosts who felt at home there once would want to stay on. I was a guest for only twenty-four hours, and I never wanted to leave.

12
MAGGIE, I HAVE YOUR BABY

O n a dark and stormy night in the late nineteenth century, a young woman named Maggie Bloxom was on her way to freedom. She was pregnant, carrying the child of her boyfriend. Excited by the fact that she would soon be a mother, Maggie also knew that her family would never approve of her having a baby out of wedlock. So, shortly after midnight, Maggie left her family home, taking a simple horse-drawn carriage as transportation. Following a dark and isolated country road through the woods in between the Sussex County towns of Woodland and Seaford, Maggie Bloxom was to meet her beloved, and then they would ride off together into a new life, soon to be a family.

Tragically, this would never come to be. Just as Maggie's carriage was crossing a lonely bridge, a huge clap of thunder exploded in the night, spooking her horse. The horse, the carriage and Maggie Bloxom herself went off the bridge and fell into the rocky creek below. When Maggie's body was found by a search party the following morning, they recoiled in horror at the grisly sight before them. Not only had Maggie Bloxom and her unborn child been killed in the fall from the bridge, but she had also been decapitated. Her severed head was found in the river, her face twisted into a mask of fear and anguish. Now she would never be able to hold her precious baby in her arms. The story goes that somewhere in the woods near Seaford, there is a lonely, abandoned graveyard where many Bloxom family members are buried. Maggie Bloxom is said to be one of them. She died young.

Maggie's Bridge
as it appeared in
January 2021.

The bridge where Maggie Bloxom died still exists today on what is now known as Woodland Church Road. It is not a creepy covered bridge like you may expect from legend—it is a simple asphalt road with a modern guardrail that crosses a small stream. However, the area remains isolated and is especially unnerving at night, dark and silent within the deep woods. It is known to all the locals as Maggie's Bridge, and the ghost story surrounding it is one that I heard often as I was growing up in Sussex County. Mindie Burgoyne, author of *Haunted Eastern Shore* and creator of the Chesapeake Ghost Tours, said of Maggie's Bridge in an interview with WMDT television reporter Brooke Butler: "This is where young people go to scare themselves."

Many brave souls have left their marks on the area of Maggie's Bridge in the form of colorful spray paint. Many of those same brave souls have driven away from the bridge as fast as they can, terrified of what they saw in the dead of the night. Here is what often happens:

For best results, you must stop and park your car on Maggie's Bridge within the witching hour of midnight and 1:00 a.m. It must be a full moon. You must turn your car off and then get out and stand on the bridge. No headlights on, no flashlights, no phones.

And then you must call out to the darkness, saying, "Maggie, Maggie, I have your baby!"

Silence. Then you may hear the unearthly but distinct sounds of a phantom horse and carriage coming down the road, coming right toward you. Then silence.

Call out again: "Maggie, Maggie, I have your baby!"

Silence. Then your attention is drawn to the woods behind you. Within the mass of dark trees, you may begin to see strange lights begin to appear, moving closer to you from the forest. If you take a photograph, it will likely be filled with ghostly orbs. Silence. You may hear a woman's scream rip

One of many instances of graffiti at Maggie's Bridge.

through the air. Silence. You may hear the quiet sound of a newborn baby crying unnervingly close to where you are standing. Or it may stay silent. You've come this far. Say it again: "Maggie, Maggie, I have your baby!" Silence. Then a shadow. A shadow coming from the trees, through the water of the creek. A shadow that appears now standing on the road in front of you. The shadow is a woman. The woman holds her own severed head in her hands. Then the headless woman starts walking toward you.

Then you probably run into your car. You lock the doors. You look out the windows. The phantom of the decapitated Maggie Bloxom has disappeared, thank god. You put your key into the ignition, ready to drive away from here as fast as you can. You turn the key.

And then your car doesn't start. Your car is dead. And then you hear footsteps right next to your car. And then the headless ghost of Maggie Bloxom claims another victim.

———— ◆ ————

IN HIS FASCINATING AND hugely influential book *The Vanishing Hitchhiker: American Urban Legends and Their Meanings*, author Jan Harold Brunvand writes:

> *In common with age-old folktales about lost mines, buried treasure, omens, ghosts, and Robin Hood-like outlaw heroes, urban legends are told seriously, circulate largely by word of mouth, are generally anonymous, and vary constantly in particular details from one telling to another, while always preserving a central core of traditional elements or motifs...Still, like traditional folklore, the stories do tell one kind of truth. They are a unique, unselfconscious reflection of major concerns of individuals in the societies in which the legends circulate.*

The state of Delaware is filled with its own chilling urban legends. The story of Maggie's Bridge is one of them. But there are more tales to tell around our campfire tonight.

———◆———

IF YOU FIND YOURSELF driving through Frankford, Delaware, as the sun begins to set, make your way toward Cat Man's Road. You will see a dirt road leading toward the woods. If you follow it, you will come to what is known as the Long Cemetery, which was named for Colonel Armwell Long. He served with George Washington during the American Revolution and was also a veteran of the War of 1812. The colonel died on November 22, 1834, at the age of eighty and was buried in what is now known as the Long Cemetery. Soon, more graves surrounded his.

In the early decades of the twentieth century, Long Cemetery became virtually abandoned. Its isolated location, almost hidden in the forest, made it extremely popular with local teenagers as a place to drink and get up to all sorts of youthful mischief. However, there was a caretaker guarding the graves of Long Cemetery. Some say his name was Leroy Hudson, but what everyone agrees on is that all the locals called him the Catman.

He was known as the Catman due to his facial features being perceived as somewhat feline. He had piercing green eyes, was tall and thin with long sharp fingernails and always wore black. Whenever a group of teenagers came to Long Cemetery at night looking to make mischief, the Catman would emerge from the darkness and chase them all screaming back to their cars.

Eventually, the Catman died. To honor his years of dedicated service to Long Cemetery, his family erected a mausoleum in the center of the

The oldest section of Long Cemetery. Colonel Long's grave is to the left of the central tree.

This empty space may have been the location of the Catman's Crypt, demolished in 1994.

graveyard and interred his remains there. This family crypt became known for miles around as the Catman's Grave.

Over the years, many people have made the journey to Long Cemetery at night, parked their cars and walked to the decaying mausoleum. Then they would knock on the bricks of the Catman's crypt three times to summon him. Many have reported seeing the dark figure of an impossibly tall man with glowing green eyes and sharp fingernails begin to stalk them through the cemetery. Then people run to their cars and the battery seems to be dead, preventing them from leaving this haunted graveyard. Sometimes their cars finally start working again, allowing them to escape. Sometimes, those who dared to summon the Catman were never seen again.

The Catman's Grave in the center of Long Cemetery no longer exists. Due to vandalism, the family had the mausoleum torn down and the bodies reinterred in unmarked graves. But there is one final bit of horror to this tale. When the workers demolished the crypt in 1994, they discovered that nearly every inch of its interior walls were covered by deep scratch marks, as if made by the razorlike nails of a monstrously large cat trying to claw its way out of the tomb.

———◆———

NEAR THE TOWN OF Felton, Delaware, in Kent County, along Highway 12, a terrible atrocity took place during the early nineteenth century. A young enslaved Black man was murdered by a White slaveowner, Michael Bonwell. Bonwell then desecrated the young Black man's corpse, dismembering it, grinding up the bones and flesh and feeding the human remains to his loyal black hound, thus making sure the murder would never be discovered.

Ever since then, people driving down this stretch of road at night have reported seeing a dog that is unnaturally "as long as a fence rail" with glowing red eyes. This is the ghostly manifestation of the murdered Black man, and this spectral hound is said to be an omen of impending death. This stretch of road is also infamous for being the site of far more car accidents than other surrounding areas, and many of these crashes are fatal. Some believe that these deaths are due to supernatural manifestations of the so-called Fence Rail Dog, a spirit hungry for revenge and justice from beyond the grave. Be careful if you drive down that road at night. Beware the big black dog with the red eyes.

———•———

NOT FAR FROM THE site of Maggie's Bridge is Airport Road, which runs through the town of Seaford, Delaware. Legend has it that one night a young woman left her house to surprise her boyfriend on Valentine's Day. She was wearing a beautiful brand-new white dress. When the young woman got to her boyfriend's house, she found him cheating on her with another girl. Distraught, the young woman ran away from her boyfriend's house and onto Airport Road, where she was hit by a speeding car and killed instantly.

Ever since then, people who drive down Airport Road after the sun sets on Valentine's Day have reported seeing the frightening apparition of the heartbroken young woman, still wearing the bloodstained white dress she had on at the time of her violent and tragic death. People driving down the road with their windows down at night have also heard sounds of a woman crying. For decades now, many witnesses have also reported stopping to pick up a young woman hitchhiker standing on Airport Road. She is wearing a white dress. She has tears on her face.

When they stop their cars and unlock their doors to let her in, they find that she has mysteriously vanished into the darkness of the Delaware night.

13

WICKED WITCHES
AND SWAMP MONSTERS

orothy Williams Pepper, who lived in Selbyville, was a Delaware
treasure. My signed copy of her 1976 book *Folklore of Sussex County,
Delaware* is as precious as gold to me. Within its pages are hundreds
of priceless historical anecdotes, folk traditions and legends that would likely
have passed out of human memory if she had not written them down. As
a native of Sussex County myself, reading her book gives me the authentic
flavor of home, preserving the world I grew up in. Pepper began writing
down folktales and stories when she was twelve years old, and she never
stopped. She was also a teacher for thirty-six years, while at the same time
contributing regular articles to the *Delaware Folklore Bulletin*. Dorothy Williams
Pepper died on September 8, 1996 at the age of eighty-five. I wish I could
have known her.

In her book, among the home remedies and colorful recollections of
ordinary life, there are of course many references to widespread belief in
the supernatural in Sussex County:

*In the 1870's, neighbors went visiting at night after the supper dishes were
washed. They ate corn popped in the fireplace and sometimes apples, since
many farmers had fruit orchards. The children played outside, but usually
ended up watching as their parents played Talking Tables. To play, four
people sat around a nightstand or a small table, touched the table lightly
with all fingers, and rubbed the tips of their fingers very lightly in a circular
motion. One hand went clockwise and the other went counterclockwise. This*

was done while all concentrated deeply on a question that had been asked. Everyone in the room was very quiet. Sometimes after long concentration, a table leg would rise up slowly, and tap out the answer. A common question asked was, "How many pigs will my old sow have?" The table leg banged eight times and, sure enough, when the pigs were born there were eight in the litter. Another question was "Will I get a letter this week? Bang once for yes and twice for no." Before too long there would be two taps. One night three of the boys, Cash, Willie, and Ed, wanted to have some fun. They crawled under the house, kept very quiet, and tapped the answers before the table moved. Talking Tables enjoyed a revival in the 1930's.

Folklore of Sussex County, Delaware also includes many tales of local witchcraft, including:

Dill Robinson was a [Black] woman who was able to put spells on people. This she did sometimes for pay and sometimes for pure malevolence. The person under the spell lost his appetite and wasted away. For a small amount, Dill could sometimes be persuaded to take off the spell. She lived in the area southwest of Bridgeville. She had refused to lift the spell from a man who had asked her to relieve him. In a state of exasperation and terror he went home and the next morning drew a reasonable facsimile of Dill's countenance, loaded his gun with silver (for witches are impervious to lead), and proceeded to shoot the picture. It is well known that this is one of the ways in which witches are subject to death, as are other mortals. Now the story is that the exact hour her picture was shot, Dill, who was riding in a carriage eight miles across country, dropped dead on the seat beside the driver. Whether or not this broke the spell is unknown.

Another notorious Sussex County Witch was Mollie Kehonk, known as Old Moll. She was an ancient hag who lived in a small cabin deep in the woods near Millsboro, and she was both respected and deeply feared by the surrounding community. Parents would always warn their children: "Stay out of them woods or Old Moll will get ya!" Whenever local children went missing in the forest, Sussex Countians would whisper that Old Moll had taken them to use in her infernal rituals of dark magic. The story goes that one day some brave boys were out in the woods fox hunting when they came across Old Moll, who said to them angrily, "Ye'd just as well go home because today ye'll catch no fox!" Laughing, Old Moll disappeared, and soon the boys' hunting hounds

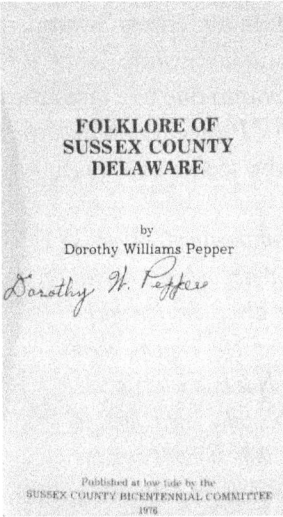

FOLKLORE OF
SUSSEX COUNTY
DELAWARE

by
Dorothy Williams Pepper

Published at low tide by the
SUSSEX COUNTY BICENTENNIAL COMMITTEE
1976

My treasured used copy of
Dorothy Williams Pepper's
incredible book, signed by her.

picked up the scent of a fox. The boys spent the whole afternoon chasing the fox through the trees, noting that it was the biggest fox they had even seen. Finally, they cornered the fox in an old elm tree and shot it. Then they heard a scream that sounded more human than animal and were shocked when they could find no trace of the fox. What they did find was the body of Old Moll "with her brain blown out."

One of the best supernatural tales related in Dorothy Williams Pepper's book continues to fascinate and frighten to this day, and she herself ended up becoming a small but vital player in the development of this indelible legend. The story is related in her book under a simple but spine-tingling heading, "The Swamp Creature."

For many years local residents, especially teenagers, have talked about a Swamp Monster. Most of the adults of Selbyville and neighboring areas thought it was a hoax dreamed up by some teenagers, or perhaps someone dressed in Halloween garb to scare people. A resident who had lived at the edge of the swamp for seventy years added that a few years ago a bear scare blew up after a game warden shot and buried some stray dogs in the area. The warden went back a few days later and found that the carcasses had been dug up and partially eaten. Claw marks were found nearby that led some people to say it was the work of a bear. No bear was found. A carload of five high school girls reported sighting a hairy, moaning creature—half man or perhaps a two-legged animal. Several others, and at least one adult, said they heard the moaning sound and saw the creature. Blood was seen on some logs near the swamp road. If you ride through the swamp, be sure to look carefully. Maybe you'll catch a glimpse of the horrible monster.

This is one of those classic local urban legends that, once born, never truly dies. Location is always crucial in spooky tales such as this, and fortunately the home of Delaware's swamp monster is an eerie place filled with history. Although much diminished from what it used to be, it is still the largest freshwater swamp on the Delmarva Peninsula, and it has gone by many names over the centuries. Currently known as the Great Cypress Swamp, it has also been known in the past as the Great Pocomoke Swamp (since it is the source of the Pocomoke River) and the Burnt Swamp due to a disastrous fire that occurred in 1930. The 1938 Federal Writers' Project book *Delaware: A Guide to the First State* does a terrific job of setting the scene, as always:

> *Originally the great "Delaware Everglades" contained thousands of acres of bald cypress timber.... Of the large old growth cypresses only a scattered few survive deep in the almost impenetrable jungle along the Pocomoke River itself, their trunks rising smooth and straight to lofty crowns, their knees standing like elves above the black water.... Big blue huckleberries are gathered by the hundreds of gallons by swamp people who know how to choose their footing... Game laws here mean no more than liquor laws; the people of the Great Swamp have run their moonshine stills for generations, and these stills are another reason why strangers have to watch their step. A causeway runs for miles through a watery waste of blackened snags—the result of the terrible fire of 1930, said to have started from an exploding still. The fire burned for eight months while hundreds of volunteers struggled to control it. They could not, because it burned underground that dry year through the accumulated peat of ages, and burst forth anywhere and everywhere, even in the middle of nearby cornfields. Not only was standing timber burned, but the destruction of the peat bed, many feet deep, meant the destruction of the buried cypress for which the swamp was most noted.... The great swamp is still here, a stubborn, melancholy wilderness whose mists rise like the ghosts of its vanished cypresses while the buzzards wheel overhead. On dark cloudy days there may be heard from the depths of the swamp, it is said, the sound of the "Old Man" riving out his cypress shingles hour after hour, as he used to do. He is a ghost, too.*

The Burnt Swamp Monster may be a genuine cryptid perhaps still living in the swamp near Selbyville. I wonder, given the reports of a ghostly man within the woods, if the monster is really the apparition of the man whose moonshine still exploded, starting the great fire of 1930. A man burned beyond all human recognition, still feasting on the blood of animals and unlucky people who dare to venture into the darkness of Great Cypress Swamp.

Whatever the monster may be, it has been encountered by numerous people over the years and up to the present day. In the 1930s, after the great fire, two men ventured into the swamp with their dogs with the intent

Deep inside the Great Cypress Swamp. *Photographed by Kej605 in 2013, Creative Commons License.*

of going hunting, but they ended up being hunted themselves. Suddenly, the dogs put their tails between their legs and began to whimper. That was when the two men heard something screaming in the dark of the swamp, something that followed them, snapping large tree branches as if they were twigs, until they reached the safety of the road.

On October 30, 2015, the day before Halloween, reporter Mark Eichmann wrote an article for WHYY that explained an intriguing chapter in the legend of the Burnt Swamp Monster with a confession by a man named Fred Stevens:

> *The legend hit its peak in 1964 when Selbyville resident Fred Stevens brought the creature to life. "I was the swamp monster 50 years ago," Stevens said during an interview near the edge of the swamp. Having grown up hearing tales of the swamp monster, Stevens, then 21-years-old, decided to cash in on the local legend. At the encouragement of his friend, local newspaper employee Ralph Grapperhaus, Stevens created a swamp monster costume using his Aunt Dorothy's raccoon fur coat. At night, Stevens would*

hide out along a road that cut through the swamp. Dressed in his makeshift monster costume and wielding a bat with railroad spikes sticking out of the end, Stevens pounced. "[I would] jump out on them. Some of them would quit before they got up to me. They'd go back down the road flying," Stevens said. Grapperhaus would publish stories of the incidents in the local paper and the legend grew. Eventually, visiting the swamp monster became a big attraction for local young people, who sometimes brought offerings to appease the beast. "Some people would come back, and they'd throw chickens toward me to feed me, I guess," Stevens said. "There was a whole mess of blood and chickens and it was quite good." He said some visitors came from as far as Dover and Salisbury, Maryland. But no amount of newspaper sales was worth the risk of this unorthodox job. "We just had to quit because so many people were coming back in pickup trucks and they were all about half drunk and they were shooting their guns," Stevens said. "Somebody will shoot you and they really didn't mean it, so we just quit, you know." More than 50 years later, Stevens still enjoys the notoriety of his swamp monster days. He's talked to lots of parents who used the legend of the swamp monster to keep their kids in line.

That raccoon fur coat Fred Stevens used as the Swamp Monster belonged to his aunt Dorothy Williams Pepper, the woman who later wrote *Folklore of Sussex County, Delaware*. It is not known if she was aware of her nephew's creepy prank. But I like to imagine that if she did know how she had inadvertently contributed to the legend, she would have found it delicious.

This does not mean that the Burnt Swamp Monster of Selbyville, Delaware, is a fiction. Far from it. Encounters continue to be reported. As recently as January 13, 2004, a student at the Delaware Technical Community College named John told the story of the night he drove down the road cutting through the Great Cypress Swamp and saw something he could not explain. Nancy Marietta related John's uncanny experience on her blog *Sasquatch Observations*:

I turned off my high beams, thinking it was a person because it was standing up. As I got closer to this being, I was taken back by its size.... This entire figure had a thick black cover of hair, with no hair on its hands....I estimate it was around 7 to 8 ft. tall. I was almost past this creature when it looked at me and then looked back to the woods as if it didn't care I was there. Once I made eye contact the hair on my arms stood up and I peeled out of the location.

The Great Cypress Swamp in Sussex County, Delaware, has twice been nominated to become a National Park, first by Senator Joe Biden in 1980 and again by Senator Tom Carper in 2004. Both attempts were opposed by the locals. They know better than anyone what still lurks in the darkened depths of the Burnt Swamp, ready to drink your blood. Be careful if you dare to explore the swamp at night. Beware. Take care. Fear the monster.

It watches you, and it waits for you, and then when you least expect it, it— *Yum, yum.*

———◦———

WHEN I SENT HER this chapter, my grandmother told me, to my surprise and delight, that she had known Dorothy Williams Pepper and her nephew Fred Stevens. I was eager to see if I could interview Fred Stevens for this book, and I asked my grandmother if she had his contact information so I could get in touch with him. An hour or so later, my grandmother called back and left me a voicemail: Fred Stevens had died just five days prior. His obituary reads, in part:

> *William Frederick Stevens, aka the "Swamp Monster" age 83, of Selbyville died Friday, January 8, 2021 at home....Fred served in the U.S. Marine Corps and retired after 34 years at DuPont Co. He designed several logos at DuPont in Seaford. Fred was the notorious Swamp Monster of the Cypress Swamp....He was the designer of the Selbyville Town Seal and the town historian and also designed the Wissahickon Tribe #20 Emblem....Fred was also a Halloween costume enthusiast who won several contests over the years. Fred was instrumental in getting state prisoners to clean Joe Long Cemetery in Selbyville, in getting a new museum for the Town of Selbyville and he worked with State Archives in presenting a monument in memory of John McCabe (Revolution War Soldier) at the Redmen's Cemetery.*

This is a stark reminder of why collecting and retelling all these tales is important. I wish I could have spoken to Fred Stevens myself, but I am grateful he did tell his story himself before he passed. Now I tell it to you, and hopefully you will remember him and the creepy Delaware legend to which he was instrumental in giving new and continuing life. Tell the tale, pass it on.

14

GHOSTLY GUARDIANS
AT OLD CHRIST CHURCH

The first time I started telling stories about history was at Old Christ Church, located near Chipman's Pond in Laurel, Delaware. Construction of Old Christ Church began in 1770 and was finished in 1772, when this section of Sussex County, Delaware, was still considered part of Maryland. On the National Register of Historic Places, Old Christ Church is one of only a dozen historic places of worship on the Atlantic coast of the United States that has never been wired for electricity or had indoor plumbing installed, nor had its interior painted or altered. It is, in many ways, just as parishioners would have experienced it in the eighteenth century.

Nicknamed "Old Lightwood" due to its weathered appearance, Old Christ Church was built with an extremely high barrel-vaulted ceiling that looks like the bottom of an enormous old sailing ship. Since 1922, the site has been lovingly cared for and restored by a nonprofit organization called the Old Christ Church League. My grandparents were members, and, on some weekends, they would be in charge of opening the church up for tours to anyone who stopped by. I volunteered to help them. I memorized the historical brochure and began to give tours of the church to visitors myself. I couldn't have been more than eleven or twelve years old at the time, but I knew somehow that I had found my calling. It was here at Old Christ Church that I began my life's work, which has led to the book you now hold in your hands.

Old Christ
Church as
seen from its
cemetery in
January 2021.

Opening up the church for tourists with my grandparents was like stepping directly into history. We opened up the big front doors, letting in the sunlight. Venturing into the vast dimness of the church, you could smell the intoxicating scent of old wood mingling with dust. Each window shutter was opened quickly, the better to let in more sunlight to the interior, displaying its simple majesty while also banishing the shadows inside. You could hear every creak in the floor, strange sounds coming from the gallery up above you couldn't identify but were forgotten once the sunlight and fresh air began to pour in to this ancient, holy and well-preserved place.

In the National Register of Historic Places nomination form dated April 13, 1972, prepared by Rea Wilkie, it is written:

Christ Church is built of wood, and so well built of fine-grained resinous heart of pine planks that is still in sound and excellent condition....Only the white window sashes are painted. The rest of the structure has weathered to the rich golden brown of old pine needles. It seems a natural outgrowth of the pine woods behind it....The wood has taken on a gratifying color from age....Several special services each year are held in the old church and people come from long distances to attend them. Regular services have been discontinued since 1850. Cherished family associations with the old church assure care of the building by staunch friends.

As I remember it, sometimes no visitors would come during the day. Sometimes there would be a handful of people, but never the number of visitors such an incredible and unique historic site deserved, or so I thought then and still do now. When people did happen to stop by, I went into tour guide mode. I would give them a brochure and show them around the church by myself. There are forty-three boxed pews that were rented by families each year. The closer your pew was to the pulpit,

A view from the church's upper gallery.
Photograph by Jacob Glickman.

the more money you paid. Many of the doors to the pews of Old Christ Church still bear the ghostly writing from parishioners' past preserved in faded chalk: family names written in elegant script, and in one instance, a hex sign or Saint Catherine Wheel was drawn on the door of pew no. 13 by someone long dead, perhaps to counteract the evil luck that comes with the number thirteen in popular superstition.

If you ascend the stairs, there is an upper gallery in the west end of Old Christ Church, where free Black parishioners, enslaved Black parishioners and White visitors or congregants who could not afford the cost of renting a pew below would sit for services on benches without backs to them. In the brochure provided by the Old Christ Church League, it says of this area:

> *Living testimony to churchgoers and visitors is two hundred years of graffiti, from the early "last of the mill" inscription over the center of the gallery to a more recent "George Washington slept here" on the west wall.*

No tour of an old church is complete without a creepy old graveyard, and after I had shown the guests the interior, the graveyard outside, surrounded by tall ancient trees, is where I would take them at the end. For a historic site that has existed for so long, there are not as many tombstones as you would expect there to be. The reason for this is that stone markers were extremely expensive in the eighteenth century. So, although only a handful of marked graves survive in the churchyard today, there are countless corpses buried under your feet whose wooden memorials have long since decayed. The most famous person buried in the graveyard is Nathaniel Mitchell. A native of Laurel, Delaware, born in 1753, Mitchell bravely fought in the American Revolution, was a member of the Continental Congress from 1786 to 1789 and served as governor of Delaware from 1805 to 1808. He died on February 21, 1814, at the age of sixty or sixty-one.

I remember vividly that in one part of Old Christ Church's graveyard, there was a small grouping of fading tombstones partially hidden by an overgrown shrub. They are all graves of children who died young, within several years of one another. This was not listed in the Old Christ Church

The gravestones of children who died young.

League brochure. It was just something I noticed. A fact that presented itself to me and has never fully left my mind. That may have been the moment when I became a historian. Many children, my age and younger, died and were buried together in a cluster. Who were they? What happened to them? What is the human history hidden behind these old stones? Those questions all still haunt me, and I'm still searching for the answers.

When it came time to close up the church at the end of the day, I remember it being a task my grandparents and I completed quickly. With every window you closed, the interior of the church became darker and darker. As shadows descended inside the barn-like chapel, I would feel uneasy. I didn't feel frightened, not exactly, but I did feel like I was not alone. That as my grandparents and I were leaving the church, something was coming back—a presence you could feel. As I walked out of the front door and into the afternoon sunlight, I never looked behind me to see what might have been watching me from in the dark among the old wooden pews. We would close and lock the front door and then go home.

Over the years since, I have passed by Old Christ Church every time I visit my parents and my grandmother. I still have tremendous affection for the place and have thought of it often. When I started writing this book, the Old Christ Church League was the first organization I contacted. Because it was where I first began to tell stories about history, I knew I wanted to include it in my first published book. I began talking with Stacy Northam-Smith of the OCCL, telling her what I was doing and my childhood memories of the church. She kindly agreed to send me a copy of the historical brochure, but then she said something that surprised and chilled me:

There are a few of us that truly believe we have a resident ghost at the church. A woman in a long black dress. I am sure there are many ghosts and spirits, but she is the one that has been seen. I will forward a picture to you next week.

Something strange appearing during a church service. *Photograph by Mary Ann Torkelson.*

I was not expecting Old Christ Church to be haunted, although looking back at my own experiences there, it made sense. The following week, as she promised, Stacy Northam-Smith sent me the brochure, along with this message: "Pictures of someone / something taken in September of 2018. This is the corner near Governor Mitchell's grave site."

The three photographs sent to me were taken by Mary Ann Torkelson during a church service. To my shock, they did not show the ghostly figure of a woman in black but something even more intriguing. In front of the church pews, a strange gathering of white light appeared that could not be explained. It gathered together and then suddenly dissipated. Perhaps another parishioner from Old Christ Church's distant past was listening to the sermon that day. Perhaps it was the ghost of Governor Nathaniel Mitchell himself, wandering in from his grave in the cemetery on the other side of the wall. When I spoke to Mary Ann Torkelson, she thought it may have been the spirit of a little girl wearing a bonnet that she had captured on film.

When I asked Stacy Northam-Smith about the ghostly woman in black, she replied:

There really are no stories regarding the woman in black except what was evidenced by myself and our OCCL president, Keith Lloyd. It was during one of our summer Sunday services. He and I were sitting on the back bench that runs the length of the wall between the two doors. Facing the chancel, I was on the right and Keith was on the left. The service had not been going long when, out of the corner of my eye, I saw a person standing in the doorway. I could not see a face but assumed it was a woman in a long black dress. The person quickly turned and went outside. I got up to invite the person to come to the service. Keith also got up and went out the other door. I went around the corner and saw no one. Keith joined me and asked if I saw someone. I stated that I did and then described the person. He saw

The interior of Old
Christ Church. *Library
of Congress.*

*the same thing. We are both sure that it was a female in a long black dress
with some sort of bonnet or veil. The board members have talked about the
woman in black as well as the vision on the wall. We have all decided that
this person, or persons, is protecting the church from misfortune.*

As of this writing, the Old Christ Church League has completed a
thorough restoration of the building's exterior. Members have also
embarked on the long and complex journey of having Old Christ
Church officially declared a National Historic Landmark. I have no
doubt they will succeed. I have visited many historic churches in my
travels through the United States, but I have never seen one as unique
and as extraordinarily preserved as the Old Christ Church in my family's
hometown of Laurel, Delaware.

May both its living and its ghostly guardians protect it for many years
to come.

THE MOST HAUNTED HOUSE
IN DELAWARE

No supernatural tour of the First State would be complete without this house located on Rehoboth Beach. It is the most haunted house in Delaware, and screams are heard echoing within its moldering walls night after night. During the day, it sits quietly by the Atlantic Ocean, and many people, young and old, pass by this haunted mansion and stare, wondering what horrors might be lurking inside. As the sun sets and the sky goes dark, those brave enough to approach this cursed place do so with fear and excitement. They have determined to go inside and explore to see if all the ghostly tales are true. Most people do not know its real history, who built it or when. To them, it has always stood there, waiting, watching the mortals walk by. Some have heard the eerie sounds of spectral organ music drifting from its broken windows. Others say the house was built on top of an ancient Native American burial ground or constructed on top of an old mine after it collapsed and that there are numerous secret passages leading to dark underground caverns. Some of the old-timers whisper that the house is occupied by the devil himself.

I am speaking, obviously, of the Haunted Mansion at the Funland amusement park, located on the boardwalk of Rehoboth Beach, Delaware. Funland's award-winning Haunted Mansion was built in 1979, six years before I was born. I can't remember how old I was when I first rode it, but I think it's safe to say I was pretty young. I've always been a spooky kid, and my parents always supported it. Growing up, there were three things you had to do whenever you visited Rehoboth Beach. First was to get a big, glorious vinegar- and salt-soaked order of Thrasher's french fries. Second, we had to get a big tub of hot, freshly made caramel popcorn from Dolle's. Last but certainly not least, we had to go to Funland and ride the Haunted Mansion. I have probably gone through it one hundred times over the course of my life, and it never gets old. I always notice something new inside the ride, and I still scream and jump every single time. To me, the only spooky dark ride I have ever personally experienced that was better than the Haunted Mansion in Rehoboth is the Haunted Mansion at Disney. I am not alone in that opinion.

For many years, Bret Malone has written and maintained the website Laffinthedark.com, the definitive location on the internet for the history of America's spookiest dark rides. He writes eloquently about his first experience with Funland's Haunted Mansion in 1999:

> *It is late evening and, while the sun begins to set in the west, a fog rolls in from the ocean. The "Mansion" as I begin to call it takes on even more of a sinister look, candles are flickering along the facade while a line has already formed in the waiting area. I purchase a fist full of tickets, and... almost silently get into the line. As I watch the now moving suspended cars begin their ascent into "God only knows what" I take a fast look up at the Buzzard. He almost seems to look angry now in the fact that I did not heed his warning. The Ghoul next to him in a broken window almost looks like he is amused at me. But, alas, no more time to worry about this as I'm now next in line. I climb into the heavy, black and cast-iron car and crash through the red doors of doom and begin the ascent upward.*

What Bret Malone captures so beautifully is the sense of anticipation Funland's Haunted Mansion provides. Unlike most of the games and rides at the park, which are nestled into only one acre of creatively used space, the Haunted Mansion does not open until it begins to get dark. Lines to experience its terrors form early in the evening, winding through a wrought-iron fence. As the natural light dims, a desiccated corpse wearing a suit of mourning black is nailed to a wooden post hanging above you. His dead mouth opens and begins to speak. The closer you get to the Haunted Mansion, the more you can hear of what he says. He explains the rules of the ride and loudly begs, "Will someone please let me down from this wall?" As your turn to enter the Haunted Mansion comes closer, you see a severed skeletonized human arm posted for children of all ages to see, warning you to keep your arms and legs inside the car at all times, or else.

The Haunted Mansion at Funland is somewhat unique in that the cars people ride in run on a track above their heads so you can't tell where you are going. This is a feature Rehoboth's spook house uses to incredible effect throughout the ride, allowing the numerous scares to register more powerfully since the riders never know when or where something terrifying might happen.

Funland, a family-run business in operation since 1962, has a fascinating history on its own. The definitive book about the park was written and self-published by author and former Funland employee Chris Lindsley in 2019. His book, *Land of Fun: The Story of an Old-Fashioned Amusement Park for the Ages*, is a great treasure and a must-read for anyone interested in Delaware history and folklore. In Lindsley's affectionate and meticulously researched portrait of the park the Fasnacht family has curated for four generations and counting, he also gives a vivid recounting of the Haunted Mansion's origins, beginning with a quote from founder Al Fasnacht:

> *We wanted this to be a family ride. We didn't want it to be strictly a teenage ride where you had people jumping out with a chainsaw and that kind of thing. We knew it was not going to be easy to put something together that would be entertaining, scary enough for a great many of the people and yet not so scary that you couldn't take your 6 year old on it.*

The majority of Funland's Haunted Mansion was built by Jim Melonic, one of the most highly regarded designers of dark rides in the United States. In Chris Lindsley's book *Land of Fun*, Melonic is quoted as saying:

> *The overhead truck and car system really helped with the design, as you can't tell where you are going unless you are looking up. When I set the tricks, I set them to draw people away from where the tricks were. So, if I had something going to jump out on the right, I would draw them to the left purposely so that it would scare them and make the ride more interesting.*

Jim Melonic's design tactics certainly succeeded at the Haunted Mansion at Funland. In the present day, there is an additional feature. At one of the biggest scares in the house, a camera pops up and takes a photograph of you. If you choose, after the ride you can buy that picture, which comes with the inscription "I survived Funland's Haunted Mansion." When I went with my partner to Rehoboth Beach for the first time in 2018, I insisted that we had to ride the Haunted Mansion together. It was his first time entering

We survived the Haunted Mansion at Funland. Will you?

the ghostly manor, and although I had explored the house many times over the years, it still managed to give me a few good scares. I bought our own "I survived Funland's Haunted Mansion" photo in remembrance.

As Bret Malone says on Laffinthedark.com:

One thing is for sure, the Haunted Mansion is not living on past hype, it is still creating a new legendary status while delivering the scares, and while Mr. Melonic did in fact create a wonderful terrifying ride, it could have just as easily started to decline over the years, much like so many rides have in history. Oh no…the Mansion still delivers due to the park's fine ownership and pride in all they do.…This is a rare example of a dark ride, that ran terrific 21 years ago, and has not lost a single step while actually improving each year due to a very caring park staff and ownership!

If you ever find yourself at Rehoboth Beach, especially if you are there with your children or grandchildren, make your way toward Funland. Buy your tickets and stand in line for the Haunted Mansion. Regard the buzzard who watches you from the roof and the burning flames in the torches that light up as the sun goes down. The little ones may be scared, and deep in your heart you might be afraid too, but you will face the horrors inside the haunted house together.

You are strapped into your black car, and then you and the child burst into the Haunted Mansion through its blood-red front door. You ascend a spooky hallway with blacklight portraits painted by Brian Allen, the artist who created the iconic and terrifying Philadelphia Flyers mascot known as Gritty. The horrors you experience together within Funland's Haunted Mansion at Rehoboth Beach, Delaware, will never be forgotten.

And you never know, that kid you took on the Haunted Mansion ride at Funland on a whim one summer night in their early childhood—that spooky-minded, quiet, shy, imaginative kid—that kid might grow up to write his own book of ghost stories one day.

———◆———

OH DEAR. IT LOOKS like our campfire just went out.

That means no more stories about the haunting of Delaware tonight. What a pity. I was just getting started. There are so many more spine-tingling tales lurking within the rich treasures of the First State's history and folklore, too many stories to tell all at once.

Perhaps you and I will meet again some other midnight, here by our campfire in these old ghostly woods. I hope we do. Until then…

It's up to you to find your way home through the darkness. Don't be afraid. Good night. Sleep tight.

BIBLIOGRAPHY

Brunvand, Jan Harold. *The Vanishing Hitchhiker: American Urban Legends and Their Meanings*. New York: W.W. Norton and Company Inc., 1981.

Burgoyne, Mindie. *Haunted Eastern Shore: Ghostly Tales from East of the Chesapeake*. Charleston, SC: The History Press, 2009.

Citron, Joel D. *Confederate Prisoners at Fort Delaware: The Legend of Mistreatment Reexamined*. Jefferson, NC: McFarland and Company, 2018.

Diehl, James. *Remembering Sussex County*. Charleston, SC: The History Press, 2009.

Federal Writers' Project. *Delaware: A Guide to the First State*. New York City: Hastings House, 1938.

Fetzer, Dale, and Bruce Mowday. *Unlikely Allies: Fort Delaware's Prison Community in the Civil War*. Mechanicsburg, PA: Stackpole Books, 2005.

George, Pam. *Shipwrecks of the Delaware Coast*. Charleston, SC: The History Press, 2010.

Healey, David. *Delmarva Legends and Lore*. Charleston, SC: The History Press, 2010.

Lindsley, Chris. *Land of Fun: The Story of an Old-Fashioned Amusement Park for the Ages*. Self-published, 2019.

Martinelli, Patricia A. *Haunted Delaware*. Mechanicsburg, PA: Stackpole Books, 2006.

Morgan, Michael. *Delmarva's Patty Cannon: The Devil on the Nanticoke*. Charleston, SC: The History Press, 2015.

———. *Hidden History of Lewes*. Charleston, SC: The History Press, 2014.

Munroe, John A. *History of Delaware*. Newark: University of Delaware Press, 2006.

Okonowicz, Ed. *Civil War Ghosts at Fort Delaware*. Elkton, MD: Myst and Lace Publishers, 2006.

———. *Spirits Between the Bays*. Vol. 1, *Pulling Back the Curtain*. Elkton, MD: Myst and Lace Publishers, 1994.

———. *Spirits Between the Bays*. Vol. 2, *Opening the Door*. Elkton, MD: Myst and Lace Publishers, 1995.

———. *Spirits Between the Bays*. Vol. 3, *Welcome Inn*. Elkton, MD: Myst and Lace Publishers,1995.

———. *Spirits Between the Bays*. Vol. 6, *Crying in the Kitchen*. Elkton, MD: Myst and Lace Publishers, 1998.

Pepper, Dorothy Williams. *Folklore of Sussex County, Delaware*. Sussex County Bicentennial Committee, 1976.

Roth, Hal. *The Monster's Handsome Face: Patty Cannon in Fiction and Fact*. Vienna, MD: Nanticoke Books, 1998.

Sarro, Mark, and Gerard J. Medvec. *Ghosts of Delaware*. Atglen, PA: Schiffer Publishing Limited, 2012.

Seibold, David J., and Charles J. Adams III. *Ghost Stories of the Delaware Coast*. Wyomissing, PA: Exeter House Books, 2000.

Vincent, Gilbert T. *Romantic Rockwood: A Rural Gothic Villa Near Wilmington, Delaware*. Wilmington, DE: Friends of Rockwood, 1998.

Williams, William H. *Slavery and Freedom in Delaware: 1639–1865*. Wilmington, DA: Scholarly Resources Inc, 1996.

Woods, Caroline. *Haunted Delaware*. Haverford, PA: Infinity Publishing, 2001.

ABOUT THE AUTHOR

J osh Hitchens was born and raised in Sussex County, Delaware. Since 2007, he has been a professional storyteller for the Ghost Tour of Philadelphia, which has been consistently rated as one of the top ten ghost tours in the United States. Josh is also a theater director, actor and playwright who has been called "Philadelphia's foremost purveyor of the macabre" and "Philly's horror maven" by the local press. His original plays include *The Confession of Jeffrey Dahmer*, which has been produced in Philadelphia, New Jersey, Canada and the United Kingdom, as well as the autobiographical one-person show *Ghost Stories*. Josh has also written and performed acclaimed theatrical adaptations of classic horror novels such as *Stoker's Dracula*, *A Christmas Carol*, *Mary Shelley's Frankenstein*, *The Legend of Sleepy Hollow* and *The Picture of Dorian Gray*. In 2010, he became the creative director at the Ebenezer Maxwell Mansion, Philadelphia's only authentically restored Victorian house museum. Josh also researches, writes and narrates the podcast *Going Dark Theatre*, which is dedicated to examining the human stories within true tales of haunted places, unsolved mysteries and horrific history from all over the world. He lives in West Philadelphia with his partner and a cat named Mina. This is his first book.

Photograph by J.R. Blackwell.

Visit us at
www.historypress.com

www.ingramcontent.com/pod-product-compliance
Lightning Source LLC
Chambersburg PA
CBHW060345100426
42812CB00003B/1127